ADVANCE PRAISE FOR
WHITE SPACE

"Jennifer De Leon chronicles with poignancy and humor the ways that she and her immigrant parents navigate everything from higher education and job searches to reproductive rights and the lasting impacts of Guatemala's civil war. This is the book I have been waiting for—a moving dispatch on family, country, and creativity from a daughter of the Central American diaspora."
—Daisy Hernández, author of *A Cup of Water Under My Bed*

"As a daughter of immigrant parents, I feel seen by these essays and the prose is stunning—they read like a blanket that I can cuddle up to underneath. *White Space* keeps us company as we ourselves face the unpredictable, straddling multiple realities."
—Angie Cruz, author of *Dominicana*

"De Leon takes the register of fierce familial love, built and held onto upon the harsh ground of dislocation like nobody else can. What is dark she illuminates, what is radiant she complicates until we are left with nothing less than the truest account possible. This is a collection not only for her ancestors and children but ours— De Leon writes a singular world large enough to contain us all."
—Ru Freeman, author of *A Disobedient Girl*

"De Leon writes with such sly power, rendering intimate family moments with humor and compassion, uncovering her identity in what was said and unsaid. The essays in *White Space* are lyrically deft and thrillingly honest, yes, but reading them what I felt most acutely was joy: the joy of watching a young woman write her way through the world and write her way into her own story, her own space of being."
—Alex Marzano-Lesnevich, author of *The Fact of a Body: A Murder and a Memoir*

WHITE SPACE

WHITE SPACE

ESSAYS ON CULTURE, RACE, & WRITING

JENNIFER DE LEON

UNIVERSITY OF MASSACHUSETTS PRESS
Amherst and Boston

ISBN 978-1-62534-567-7 (paper)

Designed by Deste Roosa

Set in Neutraface and Alegreya

Printed and bound by Books International, Inc.

Cover design by Deste Roosa

Cover photograph by OtmarW/Shutterstock.

Library of Congress Cataloging-in-Publication Data

A catalog record for this book is available from the Library of Congress.

British Library Cataloguing-in-Publication Data

A catalog record for this book is available from the British Library.

The following portions have been previously published: "Mapping Yolanda" in *Ploughshares* (2012); "The White Ceiling" in *Ms.* (March/April 2000); "Round Three" in *Generations Literary Magazine* (2010); "A Pink Dress" as part of introduction in *Wise Latinas: Writers on Higher Education* (University of Nebraska Press, 2014); "The White Space" in *Fourth Genre* (2012); "The First Day" in *Best Women's Travel Tales* (2010); "Lucky Woman" in *The Southeast Review* (2013); "A Map of the World" in *Brevity* (2013); "Work" in *Michigan Quarterly Review* (2018); "Gyms" in *Prairie Schooner* (2018); "Mother Tongue" in *This Is the Place: Women Writing about Home* (Seal Press 2017).

CONTENTS

AUTHOR'S NOTE

I grew up surrounded by stories. Yet it wasn't until the eighth grade that I began to keep a journal. It may have had to do with the fact that during the summer between seventh and eighth grade my family and I traveled from Massachusetts to California for a family reunion with my father's five brothers and two sisters and their kids and their kids' kids, along with my father's mother, my *abuelita*. In preparation for the trip, I pulled photographs of myself as a baby, a toddler, a small child, from all our photo albums at home and created a "Jenn album" which I showed off to relatives I'd never met. It was a wonderful trip in so many ways. Until the end. With my uncle's truck loaded with our luggage, we stopped at a souvenir shop in Los Angeles on the way to the airport "just to get a few things" for our family back in Boston. When we made our way to the truck, the back door hung open like a tongue. All our suitcases had vanished. All our clothes, personal belongings, my sister's Walkman, my dad's camcorder, my mother's jewelry, all of it—gone. My parents hugged us tight and anxiously looked around, as if the robbers weren't done taking what they wanted. My uncle then rushed us to the airport with only the clothes on our backs. "These are things," my mother said. "Things are replaceable. Thank God we're all okay. We'll be okay." It was then I realized that my photo album was inside my suitcase. And where was my suitcase? I would never know. Maybe this is why I began keeping a journal. I would spend my life making up for the family *fotos* that had been ripped from me in a matter of minutes.

The stories here are my own interpretations of events, told through my mind's eye and my memory's reach. The individual essays can be read separately, out of order, or sequentially, as a whole. In any case, my hope is that you, dear reader, are able to find a mirror or a window, or perhaps both, in this photo album made of words.

WHITE
SPACE

PART I
BEFORE

MAPPING
YOLANDA

O NE FRIDAY NIGHT THE winter I was twelve, tío Erwin showed up at my grandmother's apartment in Jamaica Plain with his new wife. She was fifteen. They'd met during his recent trip to Guatemala. She looked like any one of my cousins, only she didn't weigh as much. Her smile stretched, revealing teeth so white they looked like they would glow in the dark. She was short like tío and had fluffy, frizzy hair, and her skin was the same color as the outside of a loaf of bread.

"This is Yolanda," tío Erwin said. Underneath the buzzing fluorescent light in my grandmother's kitchen, he draped his arm over his bride's shoulder. They practically purred.

When I kissed Yolanda's cheek I inhaled her scent—a combination of incense and floral perfume. She tickled my chubby middle and giggled when I stood back, startled. My mom tore the lid off a box of Dunkin' Donuts and set it on the table where my aunts sat, their elbows resting on the green-and-white checkered tablecloth. "¡Niños!" she said, "¡váyanse para la sala!" We were banned from the kitchen so the women could get to know Yolanda.

The living room was crowded with mustached uncles, including tío Erwin, and my dad, who said, "*Mija*," and pushed his lips toward the kitchen. "My daughter, you should go play with your cousins."

Kids were forbidden from playing in the bedrooms too, so we were left with the linoleum strip of hallway. We cousins ranged in age from six-year-old David, a fan of Ninja Turtles, to sixteen-year-old Erika, with her feathered bangs and Guns N' Roses T-shirts. Unlike most of my cousins, I adored Barbies and Pogo balls and puffy-painted tops. My sisters, parents, and I lived in a neighborhood where the only nighttime sound was a recycle bin rattling down a driveway.

My parents agreed that education was important. It was the reason they had left their homeland of Guatemala and, later, Boston. They believed the suburbs meant security—good schools, organized sports, a library down the street. My mother pushed the idea of college on us before we could write in cursive. We took elective classes in French and read chapter books for fun. Many of my cousins, on the other hand, lived in Section 8 housing and changed schools often. But when we were all together, in the pocket of Friday night, we were the same. We played checkers and compared our favorite scenes in *The Goonies*. We played Go Fish with a sticky deck of cards. Eventually, we would teach Yolanda how to play too.

From where I sat that first night, cross-legged in the hallway next to the kitchen, I could see Yolanda's round face, mischievous grin, and nostrils wide as dimes. My grandmother sat closest to Yolanda, who was eating a Boston cream doughnut. Yolanda wore a long cotton skirt and a Celtics jacket. From my aunts' head nods and thick fingers raised in the air, it seemed someone was making a speech. I leaned closer and snatched what I could: "Uno nunca sabe . . . tiene que cuidarse."

One never knows *what? You must take care of yourself.* They hadn't said, "Be careful." That was something we constantly heard. Be careful riding the scooter and don't go past the yellow house where the Chinese family lives. Be careful swimming or you might drown like Monica almost did one summer. "You must take care of yourself" implied a further concern. If you don't take care of yourself, then _____. Whatever filled that blank space, I wouldn't know for years. *Cuídate,* "take care."

That spring we celebrated my birthday with a barbecue at Larz Anderson Park. Surrounded by shades of green, my cousins and I were allowed to be as loud as we wanted without downstairs neighbors calling the cops to complain about "them spics." I was thirteen, so I was too old to play tag. Instead, I sat at the wooden picnic table and licked the salt off Cape Cod potato chips. I placed one on my tongue and let it dissolve like the wafer at Mass. Tío Erwin showed up again, this time without his teenage bride.

"Is Yolanda here?" he asked out of breath.

My mother ripped apart a head of iceberg lettuce and arranged the leaves onto a ceramic plate. "No."

Tío massaged his temples with his palms.

"She was gone when I woke up."

Later, we found out that Yolanda had been sleepwalking. I imagined her black jelly shoe sandals swishing past the triple-decker apartments, down the concrete hill, reaching Hyde Square, and headed to the supermarket or church. These were the only places she'd find someone to speak Spanish to, someone to tell about the baby kicking against her expanding belly. After that, tío Erwin put newspapers on the rug next to her side of the bed so he'd hear if she got up in the middle of the night. Who knows where she would have wandered. My mother seemed especially concerned for Yolanda. Maybe it was because they had grown up in neighboring *colonias* in Guatemala. Or maybe she knew more than she would admit.

After the baby was born, Yolanda's mother, doña Consuelos, arrived from Guatemala to help take care of her new grandson, Jonathan. Weeks and months stretched between family get-togethers—at least for me. Most weekends I earned money babysitting, spending nights in wealthy people's living rooms. While their children slept, I tried to figure out the complicated remote controls to watch movies and eat endless snacks—Chipwiches in the freezer, Halloween candy in the cupboard all year round, pizza. I preferred the cushy tan couches, where I would talk to friends on the phone, to the crammed apartments in Boston, where my parents and younger sister still spent weekend nights with family.

The minute I turned sixteen I started working at the Gap. I learned to fold jeans diagonally at the knee. I could explain the difference between a classic and a relaxed fit. The store manager called me Maria. "Oh, sorry," she'd say, looking over my head when I corrected her. With my employee discount I could finally afford the preppy styles displayed in the storefront windows. I could fit in with the rich Jewish kids at my high school. My cousins started to call me *white girl*.

We branched out in different directions. Some of the guys took up weed and basketball or started having sex, and my girl cousins found love in the form of serious *novios*. Or they gained weight. My sister fulfilled my mother's lifelong dream and became the first in our extended family to go to college. I followed soon after, attending a small liberal arts school two hours away. College was like another country. They served food I'd never heard of (hummus), students wore clothes I didn't have (Patagonia), and professors encouraged us to call them by their first names. At least I could speak the language—the middle- to upper-class, white, privileged vernacular—or at least I could fake it by throwing in the word *vicariously* now and then. A friend "couldn't believe" I'd never heard the song "Stairway to Heaven." I couldn't believe he had only two cousins. I had thirty-eight.

Once, in World Politics, a student in the front row with a blond ponytail and high-pitched voice declared that it was unjust for ATMs in America to offer Spanish as a language option. "Why don't people just learn to speak English?" The hardwood floors and ceiling-high windows closed in, and I could feel eighty eyes on me. What did I have to say? Me, the Spanish-speaking representative in our classroom. I raised a shaking hand and said, "Sometimes it's easy to forget that the word Florida means 'flowered' in Spanish and that Colorado means 'red' or 'colored.' These are words in Spanish because the Spanish were actually here before the English. I'm just saying."

When it became too much, when I simply grew tired of having to explain *where I'm from*, or when Mexican night in the college dining hall failed to soften my homesickness, I called my mother. Cell phones had not yet infiltrated campuses, but she had a special long-distance plan that allowed unlimited minutes on the weekend. Usually she spoke in Spanish, and I used a mix of Spanish and English. When I didn't want my roommate to understand, I stuck to Spanish. My mother would ask about my classes and my friends, and she would listen with enthusiasm. She'd catch me up on the family, almost always sharing news of a pregnancy, a separation, a scandal at church. One day she called to tell me about Yolanda. I was sitting on my twin bed propped up by cinder blocks. My feet dangled off the edge, and through the window I could see that autumn had set the tops of trees ablaze in reds, oranges, and yellows.

"Listen. Yolanda called the cops on your tío the other night. She was screaming, acting crazy. Tore at her own clothes, clawed her face with her nails. Sí . . . And she told the police that your tío did it. They were going to arrest him but one of the police checked Yolanda's hands and found blood under her nails."

"Oh my God!"

My roommate walked in wearing a bathrobe and holding a dorm shower caddy. "Who's pregnant now?"

"I'll call you back," I told my mom.

That winter tío Erwin, devastated, moved from Boston to Framingham with Jonathan, who was now in elementary school. No one saw Yolanda for a long time. If the adults still talked to her, I didn't know. Eventually, we lowered our heads at the mention of her name. She became hazy in my memory, nothing like the girl who tickled my middle in my grandmother's kitchen seven years before.

If I were to draw a timeline of my parents' lives, I could see that after they came to the United States in the seventies, their lives dramatically improved. They worked hard, saved money, and in the early eighties bought their first house. My mother learned to drive. We spent nearly every weekend visiting family in Boston, but we always returned to our house in Framingham on Sunday evenings in time for my sisters and me to finish our homework. But moving to America wasn't enough to guarantee a better life for Yolanda. It just wasn't that simple. She hadn't immigrated as we had. She had disappeared.

College came to an end. Classmates left for law school, medical school, fellowships, travel abroad, or jobs in New York City. I moved across the country to work as a teacher. I could have found a position in Framingham where my sixth-grade teacher still worked and still wore a beehive. Instead, I chose California. Deep down, I wanted to experience the feeling of being from somewhere else, of reaching for something more as my parents had done.

In San Jose, my third-grade students and their families came from Mexico or Vietnam. Names like Nguyen, Tran, Le, Rodríguez, and Santiago crammed the class roster. During a parent-teacher conference one afternoon, my student Andre and his father, mother, and three younger siblings, including an infant wrapped in a lavender blanket, shared the space opposite me at the kidney bean–shaped table. Andre had the highest scores in the class. His mother wanted to know why he had misspelled Halloween on the last quiz. I wasn't sure if she was directing the question to Andre or to me.

"You know," his father said, "the price movie tickets in America too high." Andre's father was barely five feet tall. I wasn't much taller, but with heels I towered over him so I was glad we were sitting down. "For me, my wife, and six, no, seven kids." He laughed.

"We going to movies on weekend is spending over one hundred dollars."

I didn't know what to say. I tried to steer the conversation back to the Excel spreadsheet and Andre's test scores among national rankings.

"So I go Best Buy and purchase projector."

Andre's mother adjusted the sleeping infant in her arms. "What happens when a student misspells a word?"

"They must write the word ten times," I said. Who knew if it really worked?

"I go library and borrow DVDs. We play onto white wall of apartment," Andre's father said with a proud smile.

"Andre?" his mother called. He'd been playing with the other kids at the math station. "Come here and spell the word Halloween."

Andre stepped forward to display his mastery.

One week a mother cried about her husband having been deported back to Mexico. The week after that a mother fell asleep during our parent-teacher conference because she worked double shifts at night. The following month another mother asked if I could help program her cell phone in Spanish. It was barely December of that first year of teaching, and I'd already learned more about international relations than from any class in college. None of the readings on our syllabi described situations like those of my students and their families. Or like that of Yolanda. The women mentioned in our wordy textbooks were distant, statistical. Maybe that's why blond girls in ponytails so freely expressed their views on assimilation. But in those classrooms, we hadn't been discussing real people anyway, right?

I always knew that Yolanda, my parents, and other relatives hadn't moved from Guatemala to the United States for wanderlust, but it wasn't until I had moved away from Boston that I saw their stories in a different light. The flashbulbs of economics and politics had revealed realities, surely, but it was the stories of others—my students' families in particular—that began to unveil my own past, even my present.

TO MY SURPRISE, DURING one of my trips home to Massachusetts, my mother suggested we visit Yolanda. She had turned up after all, had been in the vicinity all along, but lost to us. It had been years since I'd seen her. It was Christmas Day. We arrived at her rundown apartment building in Boston. What looked like urine and grease stained the sidewalk. Cars splashed through slush puddles along the one-way avenue. The air was cold and still. Graffiti marked up the bus stop signs. I breathed through my mouth to avoid the stench from the metal garbage can. The apartment buzzer didn't sound when I pushed it. All the other buttons were cracked or missing. My mom searched for pebbles on the ground and tossed a handful up to the second floor window, the sound of keys tapping on a typewriter.

"Yolanda! Open the door. It's Dora." She hesitated. "And Jennifer. She wants to say hi."

We were buzzed in. We stepped past the glass door and climbed the stairs. The muffled sound of a television filled the carpeted hall. We twisted our bodies so a man in a leather jacket coming down the staircase wouldn't knock us over. My mother tugged the sleeve of my black peacoat and said, "We're not going to stay long. I just want to see how she is."

We stood in front of her apartment door, wiping our boots on a welcome mat that was missing the *L* and the *C*. WE OME. The door opened, and there was Yolanda, tucking her frizzy hair behind her ears. It was cut short, just above her shoulders. She'd gained weight. Maybe fifty pounds. Her red sweatshirt hugged tight around her hips, and her stonewashed jeans belonged to another decade. My mother asked if she remembered me. She nodded.

"Come in," she said in a whisper. In the living room a wide-shouldered, dark-haired man was asleep on the couch. Yolanda made no introductions or explanations. Pieces of duct tape kept the blinds down along the windowsill. The space smelled of sleep. I stood close to my mother.

"Long time," Yolanda said squinting. "Let's go in the kitchen. Oh, yeah. Feliz Navidad."

In the kitchen a little boy and girl sat on wooden chairs playing video games. The boy didn't look up, just clicked away at the neon screen. Chocolate milk splotches ran down the front of the little girl's pink sweatshirt. My mother baby-stepped her way over and slowly picked the girl up from under her arms, hugging her tight.

"My daughter," Yolanda said. "And that's my son." No one mentioned Jonathan.

Yolanda ordered them to share a seat and insisted we sit down, giving us each our own chair. Within seconds she was crying as if we'd just revealed terrible news.

"I know," my mother said. "It's okay."

I had no idea what they were talking about. Maybe I still believed I wasn't allowed to join the adults in the kitchen. Or maybe I didn't want to be part of this. It was easier, safer, to remain in the role of the child, my mother's daughter. Cowardly? Polite? I didn't know what to say to Yolanda anyway, so I stayed quiet, looked around the room. The kids wore mismatched socks. Dishes cluttered the counters. A Mass Health magnet secured a child's drawing of a butterfly to the refrigerator. I felt far away—not only from all this but, strangely, also from myself.

We didn't stay long. On our way out, my mother slipped Yolanda a twenty-dollar bill, not because she asked, but because that was and still is the kind of thing my mother does. In the car, my mother said that even with sun and rain, some fruit still falls, still spoils.

Some days after our visit with Yolanda in her cave-like apartment, I heard that she had attacked her mother who was still living with her, helping with the two new children as she had with Jonathan. Yolanda tried to stab her with a pair of scissors. The state took away Yolanda's kids and she was admitted to a mental health institution. I never saw her again.

TWO YEARS LATER I came home to Boston for good. Once home, I felt the absence of my cousins who had moved away. Some followed work—Texas, California, Indiana. Others followed war—Iraq, Afghanistan, North Carolina in between. One was serving time. Most of the girls had had babies. We were all spread out, moving farther away from that linoleum strip of hallway in our grandmother's walk-up. Even as adults, we cousins remained the children of parents who wanted more from life and who believed that moving to America would achieve it. Moving was upward—at least in our minds. Our stories might begin and end in a different place, but we inherited the belief that leaving was part of the formula for economic progress. But now I sense that the reason for departure is as important as the destination. Yolanda wasn't purely seeking more opportunities in the United States; she was also trying to escape the past.

Years later at my parents' house, I finally asked my mother to fill in the gaps of Yolanda's story, a narrative that began long before the day she had arrived in Boston. My mother was sitting at the dining room table sewing the hem on a pair of my jeans. "She was so young," she said.

I stared at the impressionist painting on the opposite wall. A café in Paris. A framed print my mother had picked up at a yard sale.

"Yolanda was only fourteen, not fifteen, when she came."

What other details, I wondered, had my mother smudged from the past?

"As a girl," she explained, "Yolanda helped her mother clean the rooms at a brothel. She'd been raped."

I was thankful for the sudden noise of the needle, stitching at a high speed.

My mother used her teeth to cut a loose piece of thread. "She was still a girl when she left for the United States with your tío. Imagine."

"How did they meet?"

"On the street."

I cleared my throat.

"Not like that. Everyone hangs out on the street there. It's not like here. Your tío was in Guatemala and doña Consuelos saw that he was a good man."

"So, that's it? A good man is hanging out on the street and you send your teenage daughter to live with him in another country?"

"Things are different there."

My uncle was a prince on a white horse—or a prince with a blue passport. Maybe Yolanda's mother hoped that sending her daughter to the United States would give her a new beginning, the kind that could even delete the past. But it hadn't. When doña Consuelos moved to Boston to help with Jonathan, she seemed only to make things worse. Her presence probably ignited painful memories for Yolanda.

"We didn't know how to help her."

I welcomed the hypnotic hum of the sewing machine. We have no control over the circumstances into which we are born. The ropes we reach for in trying to soar somewhere new, somewhere better, often carry us to unpredictable places. How would Yolanda's life have played out had she never left Guatemala, how would my mother's have turned out if she hadn't either? In all the stories she told about the small Central American country that would be the source of comparison for everything my sisters and I ate, wore, and read, she was teaching us about the world and to appreciate what we had.

"Here." She handed me the jeans and placed her elbows on the table the way my aunts had done that first night Yolanda had arrived at my grandmother's apartment in Boston.

"Thanks," I said.

As I folded them at the knee, I could just see Yolanda with her frizzy hair, seated at another table somewhere, playing cards in a pale-painted room, and with her mischievous smile saying, "Go fish, go fish."

But I did not want to wait to see what cards I was dealt. Instead, I was determined to choose my own.

THE WHITE CEILING

I T WAS AUGUST 1998. The waiting room was a circus. Young mothers read *Parenting* magazine while young fathers chased toddlers wearing Nike high-tops. Abortion, birth control, and pamphlets about sexually transmitted diseases rested on the small, square wooden tables. As I checked in to the gynecologist's office, the woman behind the counter asked me why I was there. I said, "I want to go on birth control."

She asked, "Are you pregnant, honey?"

I coldly repeated, "I'm here to go on birth control." I turned away while the woman made lunch plans with her coworker.

They didn't realize this was the biggest step of my life. Latinx culture is mostly Catholic, and thus premarital sex is out of the question. Birth control? An even greater taboo. I was stuck in a glue made up of my feminist ideals mixed with my traditional Latinx values. I stood there and thought, oh God, I can't believe I'm really doing this. My mother would kill me if she knew where I was. The nurse brushed me off with an "Alright, we'll call you when we're ready."

I persisted, "I'd like for you to switch the billing address please, to Connecticut College."

"Why?"

"Because that's where I go to school."

"You mean you're in college?"

At this point I was ready to leave the clinic, just drive away. It wasn't worth the humiliation. But I knew that as soon as I got to the first stoplight I'd regret it. Who would be the one losing? Yes, I'm in college. And I'm Latina. And I want to go on birth control. What's the problem, lady? And you better believe you are sending the bill to my college address and not to my home address.

Sending the bill home would mean a war in my house. Machismo versus feminism. I was in love with someone, but I was doing this because I was in love with myself. Damn it, I was determined *not* to be the umpteenth teenage mother in my extended family. So I swallowed my frustration and waited to be called. I was terrified that someone I knew would see me.

My family and their friends always told me that birth control was bad. And if someone discovered that I was on the Pill they would think, Oh, she's on the Pill, hmm . . . she has sex . . . she probably does it with everyone because she's on birth control. Oh, her poor mother.

"Jennifer." I was up.

The nurse led me to a small room with a scale where she discussed my chart with another nurse. Finally, one told the other to explain that I needed to give a urine sample. I didn't understand why she didn't just tell me that herself. I think they noticed my confused expression, and that's when one asked, "¿Hablas inglés?"

A nurse then led me into another small room containing an examination table with stirrups. I was frightened. I had been waiting nearly an hour when a woman walked in and told me she was basically a gynecologist-in-training. When I requested a real doctor, she brought in a male gynecologist. Wonderful.

The white tissue paper began to crumple underneath me, and I lay there on the table under the sobering light, surrounded by white walls and my heavy conscience. I thought to myself, this is why. This is why so many young Latinas don't get birth control. It's an altogether unfamiliar and uncomfortable experience. There are too many walls to break down. Making the appointment over the phone when your parents aren't home (and not giving a return number for confirmation); driving to the clinic and feeling humiliated, ashamed, and doubtful in the waiting room; and *then* making it into the exam room where the staff continues to patronize you. Finally, you lie there uncertain of what is going on, hearing terms you've never heard outside of sex-ed. All this trouble for something I was taught I shouldn't be doing in the first place. This is why so many of us find ourselves in the same position, under the same white ceiling, later—when it's too late to get birth control. Yet, I wanted a different path. And so I chose it. So I thought. This is where the story ended for me, supposedly. A girl defies her cultural expectations and goes on birth control.

But it is not how the story ended.

Two months after this memorable doctor's visit, my parents and younger sister came to my college for Fall Weekend. It was Saturday afternoon at this point, and we'd just had a great lunch under white tents that had been set up on the campus green overlooking the ocean. My father and sister decided to take a walk in the arboretum while I worked on a French paper at the desk in my dorm room. Mom took a nap on my bed. Again, so I thought. A few minutes later though, she pulled a piece of paper from her purse and handed it to me. I opened it slowly. As soon as I saw the apple logo from U.S. Healthcare my stomach dropped. I knew it was the bill. As in *the* bill. My immediate reaction was shame, and I began quietly crying. After all the barriers I had tried to break, the clinic failed me. But to my surprise the feminist in my mom came out: she told me she was proud of me, that despite her wanting me to wait until I was married, she was glad I was making mature decisions for myself. I was stunned. It took me a while to make eye contact with her, but when I did, I knew she was telling the truth. And that's when I realized I'd been holding my breath and finally exhaled.

After that, I became more comfortable (as comfortable as one can ever be) going to the gynecologist—a different one, of course. I guess having my mother's approval granted me a courage I wished every Latina could have. My father? He'd read this story eventually.

Again, this is where I thought the story ended.

And again, I was wrong.

Almost a year later, I was sitting inside an internet café in Paris where I was studying abroad for the fall semester. An editor at *Ms.* magazine in New York City, where I had interned that previous summer, asked if I had any ideas for a column they ran at the back of each issue. Personal essays. Stories of overcoming adversity. Things like that. I thought, of course! The story of going to the clinic for birth control rushed to my mind. I wrote the editor. She replied immediately: *Yes, yes, yes! Send me one thousand words by Friday?* From having interned at the magazine, I knew what a big deal this was. The editor even shared that I would be paid one dollar per word. Amazing, right? I was nineteen. This would be my first published piece in a national—international!—magazine. My writing dreams would come true! But the cloud of shame came over me while seated in that café in Paris, and I knew I couldn't do it. Write about going to the gynecologist to get birth control? Out myself like this? My mother? My family? Yeah, right.

One night that week I called my mother from my home stay in Paris. As always, I used an MCI calling card. She picked up, and just the sound of her voice at home, thousands of miles away, made me miss her even more. "So, an editor reached out to me," I explained. She perked up. She listened with great enthusiasm and support and encouragement, until I shared the topic I was interested in writing about, and that's when she went silent. I knew it was too much. It was one thing for her to support me secretly, but this story would now be in print. Permanently.

"Forget it," I told her. "I'm not going to do it. There are other things I could write about. Maybe for another issue. Later or something."

She cleared her throat. "No," she said.

What?

"No, I think you should do it."

"You do?"

"Why not? It already happened. And your story could help others."

Once again, the feminist in my mother came out, loud and clear. And I, her daughter, would write about that too.

ROUND THREE

I CUT FIFTEEN INCHES OFF my hair, packed too many pairs of shoes, and amputated a tire from my twelve-speed bike before sliding it into the backseat of my best friend Steph's Toyota Corolla. We fit the rest in the trunk. I was on my way to Cape Cod for the summer. It was something I felt writers did—travel, write. I was nineteen. I didn't say goodbye to my father.

"How did you convince him to let you go?" Steph asked.

"I didn't. I left a note," I told her as I dug for a cigarette in a pack I'd owned since the winter formal at my college. Moments later I flicked the butt out the window. But did it actually make it out the window? For the rest of the two-hour ride from Boston, I was convinced I could smell my clothes burning in the backseat. I'd stuffed them in a black trash bag, along with books that seemed *writerly* at the time: Naomi Wolf, Henry Miller, Dalai Lama.

Ours was the tiny bedroom in the attic. Megan, the main tenant, had just painted the walls and angled ceiling an Amazonian green. I imagined falling asleep underneath a huge tropical leaf.

"Where are the beds?" I asked.

She explained that the former tenants took their mattresses with them, and didn't I know to bring my own, or at least a futon? *Futon.* There's a word that had not yet celebrated its first birthday in my vocabulary. It belonged with other college words, like Nalgene and hummus.

"I'm going to Bradlees," she said. If you need anything, there's a Stop & Shop down the street." Megan was pretty. But it was lost underneath her layered T-shirts, died-from-a-box red hair trapped in her ponytail, and general old-woman-in-a-shoe demeanor. She was twenty-two.

Two weeks before, when I had asked my mother if I could live on Cape Cod for the summer, she shook her head once before returning to her three-way phone conversation with my *tías*. She was scrubbing the remains of frijoles off the pan in the sink. I recognized that look. I'd seen it before when I asked if I could go on the school French Club's trip to Québec City, when I suggested I do community service for the summer in Zimbabwe, and the time I proposed the idea of spending prom night "at a friend's house." It was the look that told me, "Ask your father." Yes, the number-one hurdle to all fun stuff: dad.

"No," he said.

Round one.

"Why don't you work at a restaurant? There's the Friendly's down the street. You can walk," he added later. Of course he would say that—the thought of having his daughters too far away for too long for no reason just didn't make sense. This wasn't a semester abroad. This was summer. And I had a perfectly fine room under their roof. But I had already tasted freedom at that point, and the thought of going back to my childhood bedroom, even for a summer, made me feel like I had hives all over my body. And I wanted to write, by the ocean and stuff. So . . .

Round two.

I asked, "What if you and mom come with me to check it out first? We could go Memorial Day."

He was silent, which we both knew meant *maybe*. Monday, a holiday, round three.

My mom, dad, sister, *abuela*, and I climbed into our navy blue caravan for the never-ending drive. Up until then, the only side of Cape Cod I'd experienced had been with my family—which meant day trips to Hyannis where we'd meet up with our cousins and their families at the McDonald's to use the restroom by the rotary before the bridge. The men would go buy a bucket of worms at the fishing shack next door while the women unwrapped tinfoil and fed us tortillas and refried beans inside the McDonald's. *But we're at McDonald's*, we'd whine. Sometimes Mom would give in and buy us a breakfast platter that came on a Styrofoam platter. My sisters and I would split into thirds the sausage patties, home fries, and pancakes. The grown-ups always had coffee.

That day in the car on the way to the Cape, not once did I ask dad to change the radio station. When my thirteen-year-old sister asked to switch seats so she could look out the window, I didn't complain. Finally, we pulled up to the cottage, and mom commented, "Qué nice." Dad took his time shutting off the engine, setting the emergency break, locking the doors, checking that the doors were indeed locked, and scanning all 360 degrees, as if burglars and rapists would crawl out from behind the tall trees shielding us from the brilliant summer sun.

Megan greeted us at the screen door with a fat cat overflowing in her arms. "Hi," she said.

Mom did all the talking after that. "Hello, yes, we're from Guatemala, we used to come to Cape Cod for day trips all the time, yes, the seventies, oh wow, the kitchen, so there's laundry in the basement, okay, and how will you split the bills, oh, oh, utilities included, did you hear that?" she looked at my grandmother.

While mom was in Betty Crocker mode, dad remained silent. Same cute house, same carpeted kitchen, but dad saw only the empty beer bottle in the recycle bin, the pathetic lock on the door, an unsafe highway nearby where I'd be roadkill before receiving my first paycheck from the Lobster Pound Restaurant (assuming I'd even get the job), and the killer: Megan's boyfriend.

"Hey." The boyfriend pushed mute on the remote control and offered us a single head nod.

"Good afternoon," my father said like a general, like it was his house, like I was the girlfriend and not Megan. Like we had known them all for more than fifteen minutes.

I observed the scene through my father's eyes: low-hanging jeans, dirty sneakers, a goatee. So I suggested we look at the back porch. After that we toured the rest of the house, discussed rent, and flipped through pages of the Cape Cod Community College calendar on the refrigerator. We named dates like it was going to happen, like I'd finally be in the company of college kids across America who got to do what they wanted for the summer and not the daughter of Guatemalan immigrants who wanted their daughters to embrace the good of America—the education, the work ethic, the social values, but not if these came with tattooed boyfriends. I heard it all the way home.

"That guy is no good. He's probably there all the time." Dad caught my eye in the rearview mirror. "Don't roll your eyes at me, I say." He steered around the rotary, over the bridge. And in a tone reserved for the worst of crimes, he added, "And they drink." Had he known how I spent 100 percent of my Saturday nights my freshman year in college? How my liver practically winced at the thought of another vodka and dining hall juice concoction?

Mom changed the subject, something about a bat mitzvah for one of kids of one of the families she cleans houses for in one of the wealthy towns that start with W—Weston, Wayland, Wellesley. These are the kids my parents wanted me to be like in some ways—good grades, well-mannered, ambitious—but not in other ways—smoking pot, having sex, and constantly wanting to move away from home. How ironic, I thought, as we pulled back into our own driveway, having left Cape Cod behind like garnish at a buffet. When dad was my age, he left Guatemala and moved to another country. I just wanted to live near the beach with my best friend and go back to college in the fall and tell everyone how awesome Cape Cod was and how I would probably go back next summer. I wanted to be like the Nalgene-carrying, trust-fund-dipping, hummus- and pita-eating girls.

Dad said no. But I left anyway.

A MONTH INTO MY *awesome summer* I barely had half a journal full of writing, and my quads ached from all the biking to and from my three jobs. The Lobster Pound had decided to go with someone

else. Maybe someone less "Mayan looking," as one of my custom-
ers at Mitchell's Bistro on Route 6 had called me. The couple had
just returned from a vacation to Costa Rica. They'd bet on what
my heritage was, and the wife said, "We guessed Mayan, now
is that right? We just spent the winter in Costa Rica. Absolutely
beautiful down there. We love Central America." They left me a
two-dollar tip.

At the Phoenix Fruit Market, I separated cremini from shiitake
mushrooms, Sicilian from Italian eggplants, and a whole hell of a
lot of peaches and tomatoes. I picked up new vocabulary: almond
butter, organic, and shrooms (not the kind sold in the store). In
the mornings, when I arrived at work by half past six, the first
thing I did was step into the walk-in freezer. I watched the steam
from my arms rise into the cold air, against the crates of blueber-
ries and rhubarb. I thought of my father. How he'd grown up on
a coastal farm in Guatemala, how he'd worked so hard his whole
life, like hard physical labor. And here I was, working hard too,
but it wasn't the same.

My third and final job was working as a nanny for a family
who "summered" on the Cape in their very own beach house with
their very own outdoor shower. The little girl liked a pink bubba
(strawberry milk in a bottle), and the little boy liked a brown bubba
(chocolate milk in a bottle). We played in the sand and I took them
on "hikes" to the beach, taking the long way so they'd get tired out
and so I could stare at the ocean. I talked to mom on the phone on
Sundays. I had not spoken to dad once. Neither one of us budged.
My sister asked if I got to go swimming every day. "Yeah," I lied.

The last weekend of the summer, when bike riding and living off tuna fish sandwiches had lost their charm, I cleaned the kitchen hard. It's the way all women in our family cry. I was bored. Writing didn't come as easy as I'd thought it would, especially for living in such a beautiful place. Besides, I missed my family and friends. My bed. My best friend was now my best enemy (turns out sharing a bathroom and groceries was not at the top of our list for having an *awesome summer*). I counted the days for sophomore year in college to begin. Mom called and said that she and my tía and my sister were on their way to visit and pick up some of my belongings. I wondered if dad was coming too, but I didn't ask mom. A couple hours later, I heard the tires crunching on the long gravel driveway. I rinsed a sponge in the sink, watching the drops hang onto the foamy edge before dropping one by one into the black belly button of the sink. I placed the sponge under a spot of sun on the counter. Before I pivoted to open the front door, judging from the time it took for the tires to come to a full stop, the engine to settle, the doors to open, I'll admit it, I stood in anticipation for the sound: unlock, lock, lock. I knew from the sounds that it was him. My father was here.

A PINK DRESS

SPRING OF MY SENIOR year in college I needed to buy a dress for graduation. Not just any dress, of course. "*Vaya*," my mother, had said. So we drove to the mall, our special mother-daughter terrain. We were experts at tracking discounts. Tuesdays were retail markdown days. The salespeople at Macy's gave out coupons. And twice a year, if you purchased full-price bras at Victoria's Secret, you got a free lip gloss. That day, weeks before I would be the second in my entire extended family to graduate from college, my mother and I had a clear goal: find the dress.

There it was, underneath the soft lighting bulbs inside Ann Taylor. Magenta, magical. My mother and I gazed at the silk fabric through the storefront window. A headless mannequin showed off the exquisite A-line cut. Sleeveless, sophisticated. Nothing but a pane of fingerprint-proof glass parked between us. We stepped inside the store and were greeted by the sweet smell of leather and cashmere-blend tops as the aura of credit card transactions hovered around us like a mist.

"How much?" my mother asked.

I massaged the crisp white price tag between my thumb and forefinger.

"How much do you think?"

We left the mall that day defeated. The dress cost one hundred dollars, well over what we could afford. I was a scholarship student at Connecticut College, a private liberal arts school that resembled a country club. My mother worked as a housekeeper. I made six dollars an hour babysitting for families near campus. I would need to buy a suit for upcoming job interviews, not to mention outfit an apartment in Boston where I planned to live with two friends from college come September. My mother and I, expert shoppers, knew storefront items wouldn't be marked down for weeks, maybe months. Graduation was in seventeen days.

"I'll find a dress at the mall near school," I assured her, my voice rinsed of confidence as I pictured the crowded racks inside the mall in New London. She pursed her lips, lowered her lashes.

My college graduation dress was as important to her as a wedding gown. Ever since my mother was a schoolgirl in Guatemala, where she had often carried the flag in the annual school parade (an honor for the students with the highest marks in each grade), she had dreamed of going to college. Education was like a religion in our household. She preached the importance of straight As. She snuck in *consejos* like mashed-up vitamins in our morning mosh: "If you study hard you can get a good job, and then you can do whatever you want," she'd say, or "Books are your friends." When she was driving my sisters and me to gymnastics or Girl Scouts or church and we couldn't escape, she'd tell us about a family whose house she cleaned, how the son went to Duke (the name made me think of a prison) and how he got a scholarship (the word sounded like a disease).

Thanks to my mother's persistence, I eventually learned the meaning of a scholarship when I earned one to attend Connecticut College. One semester she spoke to my Women and World Studies class. Seated at the far end of a rectangular wooden table in the snug classroom of an ivy-covered campus building, my mother crossed her arms and described her experience moving from Guatemala to the United States at the age of eighteen, and we discussed the ways in which globalization played a role in our family's economic, political, and cultural trials. I got an A.

She also visited me at the offices of Ms. magazine in New York City where I interned one summer. I'll never forget the moment that Gloria Steinem's long-fingered, delicate hand knotted with my mother's coarse, nail polish–chipped hand—just for an instant. "How lovely to meet you," Ms. Steinem said. "You too," my mother replied. The next fall, when I studied abroad in Paris, my mother came to visit. She insisted on taking pictures of the small cars she said looked like sneakers and then asked me to take photos of her posed in front of them. In between visits to the Louvre and the Sorbonne, where I was taking a feminist philosophy class and attending lectures by Hélène Cixous, my mother bought miniature replicas of the Eiffel Tower for relatives in Boston. Throughout the years she held tight the picture in her mind of each of her daughters on that all-important day: graduation.

THE FINAL WEEKEND BEFORE college graduation, my mother came to visit me. She had packed a weekend bag and drove the two hours to campus. By now she knew where to park and how to type in the seven-digit code required for entering the dorm. There, inside my room, she relaxed on the purple comforter (the one that she had sewn herself) and talked to my grandmother on the phone while

I wore headphones and worked on a final paper. That night we ate dinner in Mystic, a quaint seaport town fifteen minutes away. We sat upstairs in a restaurant overlooking the bridge, where we ordered piña coladas and split an entrée of stuffed scallops. Afterward, back on campus, we drank frothy beers from plastic red cups and met up with my friends. By then they knew and loved her. The following morning, my mother and I ate brunch in the dining hall and then took a long walk in the school arboretum. Before she returned home, she handed me a department store bag full of hair gel, toothpaste, shampoo, and raspberry-flavored Fig Newtons. I stood on the concrete steps to the dorm and watched her drive away, the car a little lighter, both of our hearts a bit heavier. I could tell she was already mourning her visits to Connecticut College. Monday passed. Tuesday. Finally, on Wednesday morning of my last week of classes, I dug in my closet for a shirt to wear to my final presentation in women's studies. There, tucked between a sparkly tank top and a white button-down, I felt the crinkle of a cream-colored plastic garment bag. I pulled it out gently and immediately recognized the magenta fabric peeking out the bottom. I didn't have to look because I already knew what was inside.

THE WHITE SPACE

Luis De Leon

OBJECTIVE
(describe career objective here)
123 Summer Road, Framingham, MA 01701
(555) 555-5555
email account and email address forthcoming

EDUCATION
Colegio Valle Verde
55 Avenida 5–55, Zona 5
Tel: 5555–5556 Fax: 5555–5557

PROFESSIONAL EXPERIENCE
Raytheon Company
123 Boston Post Road
Sudbury, MA 01776
(555) 555-5558

PRODUCTION SUPERVISOR   *1976–Present*
- Responsible for maintenance and production of machinery and products
- Provided support and addressed the day-to-day process challenges
- Communications specialist with Spanish- and Portuguese-speaking clients and workplace engineers

SKILLS
- LANGUAGES: Spanish, Portuguese, English
- MECHANICAL: Skilled in maintenance and repair of machinery (plumbing, electric, small home appliances)
- Landscaping, roof repair, window, wallpaper, rug, and tile installation

T IS TEN O'CLOCK at night on Thanksgiving at my parents' house, and I am ready to go home. As I hold leftovers in my hands and wear my black winter coat like a cape over my shoulders, my father asks if I can help him write a résumé—the first in all his fifty-six years. I squint at him. A fold crackles in the warm tinfoil mass wrapped in a Shaw's plastic bag.

"What?" I say without taking off my coat. Besides, I have been here seven hours—no, eight—and he asks me to help him as I am just steps from the door that leads to my car that leads to my apartment in the city and my life muted from the sounds of his disapproval.

"I need to make a résumé," he says. He is slouched in his recliner in the living room.

I step back into the heart of the house, the kitchen, and place the leftovers on the oval wooden table, next to forgotten folded napkins with images of smiling turkeys and fall foliage. Smudges of cranberry sauce stain them.

"What do you need a résumé for?" I ask, slipping my arms inside my coat sleeves, threatening to leave.

It has been three years since he worked, since the cancer, since his emergency splenectomy when the surgeon told us the lymphoma had consumed his entire spleen and, *thankfully*, it is not an organ we need. Then the doctor told us the cancer had spread to his stomach and they had to *clean that up* and *staple the rest*. My mom joked that dad had scored a free stomach stapling and look how lucky he was. I suppose that was one way to look at the situation, even though his extra twenty pounds would never warrant such an operation.

"I need a résumé for this company that helps people get jobs," my father explains, facing the television.

"Oh, a temp agency?"

He turns his neck, gives me a dirty look, and I wonder if he knows what a temp agency does. I immediately feel bad for throwing in an esoteric term.

"Can I do it tomorrow?" I'm good at this game. I make promises to my parents I never intend to keep. "Oh, I'll write Mrs. Kreiner a thank-you note for you this weekend," or "I'll help you get that form notarized next week." Sometimes I do write the notes. Other times my procrastination pays off and they forget to follow up with me. My parents can speak English. They can write in English too. Fluency in a second language, however, is about more than the ability to translate one word to another. It is an invisible, yet potent comfort in the culture of that language. It is why my father is asking me for help tonight.

"I promise, I'll write it for you tomorrow."

"No," he says softly and stands up.

I spot my silhouette in the bay windows in the living room. My parents' house mirrors the other ranch-style homes along their suburban street where homeowners take good care of their lawns even if they can't afford landscaping services. Holiday lights and wreaths decorate doorways and one-car garages. The mailman always delivers an extra Value Pack coupon book per my mother's request. Neighbors pronounce my father's name as *Lew-ee* instead of Luis. I call it *our* house even though I have never lived there. My parents downgraded homes after my sisters and I moved away to Dallas, New York, San Francisco, and Boston, after a lifetime of the two of them working hard to upgrade incomes, education, health, and, of course, countries.

"Fine," I mumble like a twelve-year-old girl and not like a twenty-eight-year-old woman. I hang my coat over a kitchen chair.

My father rushes into the bedroom and returns holding a blue Post-it pad, the kind with lines. The sight of his careful cursive writing in black pen is like a stab in the heart. It pulls up memories of birthday cards where my mother would write several sentences and he would sign only his name. On the Post-it pad, I see the words: spray painter, computer parts, 1985, industrial machinery. I resist the urge to ask him who helped him with this; I hate that the question swells in my mind. He must know what I am thinking because he says, "I just started writing some things down."

I nod, avoiding eye contact.

He has time for list-making nowadays. My mother is the breadwinner now. I wonder what he thinks about the fact that his primary duty each day is to make a pot of rice for dinner.

"I brought my laptop, so I'm just going to cut and paste my résumé to a new document and change it with your information," I say.

I can tell he is excited because he shuts off the TV in the living room.

I continue. "Then I'll save it on my flash drive and put it on your computer and print it from there." His eyes widen behind his nonprescription glasses, the ones he bought at CVS on one of those plastic turning racks. I pull up the file on my laptop. Two pages. Ten-point font in Garamond. The compartmentalization of my life by internships, GPAs, university degrees.

"That's your résumé?" He points.

I minimize the screen and open a new blank document.

"It's good," he says with a wheezing sound in his throat.

"Let's start with the basics," I say to him.

We are seated at the kitchen table where my laptop adds to the clutter. I puff up the margins to 1.5 inches, change the font to thirteen-point Times New Roman (after having carefully considered Courier New), and we begin.

WITHOUT CELL PHONE OR fax numbers, email or website addresses, the top of the page looks lonely. Where do I write that my father grew up along the southern coast of Guatemala where his father worked for the U.S.-owned United Fruit Company (UFC) that helped kick communism to the world curb while pretending to care about Guatemalan citizens' intake of bananas? They were interested only in profits and maintaining a capitalist economy.

My father remembers the powdered milk and banana coloring books the United Fruit Company gave workers and their families. When my father was three years old, in 1954, the CIA organized a coup d'état to overthrow Guatemala's democratically elected President, Jacobo Árbenz Guzmán. Apparently, el señor Guzmán had implemented a number of new policies too radical for the taste of the UFC, ones that required private corporations to share their unused, unfarmed land with peasants. The UFC hadn't liked that and ran home and told its mother, the U.S. government, that Guatemala had used a bad word: communism. Eisenhower agreed that a Soviet-smelling downstairs neighbor probably wasn't a good thing, so began a forty-year civil war, complete with U.S.-trained death squads, torture, disappearances, mass executions, and over two hundred thousand Guatemalans murdered in the process. What this meant for my grandfather: get a new job. Being linked with the United Fruit Company only made him a target for the guerrilla groups.

Where do I write that in the midst of the political battles, my father's parents were engaged in their own family battle, resulting in a separation? My grandmother and her eight children—my dad was number three—were forced to move to the capital so the oldest ones could find work in chicken factories and sweatshops. Meanwhile, my grandfather wandered around the country like a bachelor. Twenty years old, my father traveled through Mexico and crossed the border in Tijuana, lived in Los Angeles briefly, before moving to Boston (temporarily) for a job he would have for the next three decades. Where do I put on my father's résumé the address of my parents' first apartment in Jamaica Plain? Or the house they bought before they turned thirty? The rooms they fought to fill with objects my sisters and I desperately wanted: Cabbage Patch Kid dolls, Nintendo, a computer? Why does the term *permanent address* suddenly seem so sparse?

I IMAGINE ASKING MY father the following: "What do you want to do?" or "What is your career goal?" I might ask, "What is the name of the specific job for which you are applying?" None of these seem right. How can I phrase the question in a way that won't make my father feel more anxious, desperate, or fearful that he can't ever get a job again? Am I the one who is paranoid, protective, and parental?

I can hear my mother laughing in the family room. No one else is home, so she must be on the telephone. I am the daughter who lives and works in Boston. I am the one who fills obligatory roles, ranging from picking up an aunt at the airport and depositing her in my grandmother's apartment living room to spending Thanksgiving with my family because it's a thirty-minute drive for me. My sisters' attendance requires transport at thirty thousand feet, an expense better saved for flights home for Christmas, a real holiday.

Finally, I find a way to pose the question to my father. "So, what is the name of this temp agency?"

He flips through the Post-it pad and points. I type in the objective: to obtain a position within the S & S Temp Agency. I want to type: to obtain a position within society that values the work of an immigrant, a husband, a son, a brother, a cancer survivor, a father, a smart and humble man who only wants to do more on weekdays than watch *The Price Is Right* while simmering rice.

ON MY OWN RÉSUMÉS over the last ten years, phrases like "terminal degree," "academic honors," and "double major" are arranged neatly under the canopy of this section. But I can't use any of these terms here. My father was denied the opportunity to complete secondary school in Guatemala because he needed to help support his brothers and sisters. Instead, he plucked feathers off dead chickens in a small factory in Guatemala City from the time he was fourteen years old. Aside from cramming for the U.S. citizenship exam in 1983 and studying diagrams in Bob Vila home repair books borrowed from the public library to figure out what was wrong with a toilet, a stove, the boiler, or the roof, my father was not "the school type."

My father hadn't inhaled the chalk and pink eraser smells of a classroom since grammar school during his childhood, when meat was cooked only on Sundays. My mom is the one who attended back-to-school nights at our elementary, middle, and high schools. When, in the early nineties, my parents signed up for a weeknight General Educational Development (GED) test prep course at the local vocational high school, my dad attended just the first class. He said it was dumb. What was dumb about it? My sisters and I had wanted to know. My mom attended each class, returning home to our small kitchen on Tuesday and Thursday nights after nine, showing off her spiral notebooks filled with algebraic formulas and multisyllabic vocabulary words. After she passed the GED exam, she borrowed my sister's high school graduation cap and gown and had professional photos taken of her at the Sears portrait studio. She showed that portrait to anyone who had eyes. My father, on the other hand, never returned to class.

So tonight, as I help my father write his first résumé, I struggle to find words to fill this white space. My laptop feels warm on my fingertips. I exhale and feel like I am failing him. What *do* I write? Suddenly I remember the look on my dad's face when he woke at 2:00 a.m. one night to get a glass of water in the kitchen. I was studying for a French midterm exam at the kitchen table. Color-coded index cards stretched in each direction. *Je veux. Je voudrais. Je ne voudrais pas.* He had scratched his head and looked at me suspiciously, as though he couldn't decide whether I was really studying or if I was doing something illegal. He eyed the flashcards and lifted his chin, his eyes heavy with a lifetime of limited sleep. Finally, he returned to bed. In that moment, I felt myself floating away from him, like I was bobbing on a raft that was inevitably headed to some other shore.

"Put that I got my high school diploma in Guatemala," my father says.

So I do.

I TRY TO FOCUS on the thirty years of labor he gave to factories where my father's shifts required him to leave and return to the house in the dark. Among his five brothers and two sisters, my father was the only one who braved New England weather long enough to believe thirty degrees Fahrenheit was a good thing. The others live in California and Texas and visit only during the summer months unless they are coming to show their children something white and cold and mean: snow.

My stoic father had a reliable (until he got cancer), old-fashioned 7:00 a.m. to 5:00 p.m., Monday–Saturday job. He is not ready to retire or perhaps unable to stomach the idea of forced retirement, so a job, any job, is what he is seeking now. Even my mother can't drive to work fast enough these days. Her role as my father's care-taker has made her eager to leave the house even if she won't admit it. How ironic that while growing up, I always thought parents hated having to go to work. Maybe they did then, but these days my parents ache for a reason to rise.

When my dad first felt sick, he did not tell anyone. One winter morning, he rose to the 6:00 a.m. alarm and was showered and dressed for work by 6:30 as usual. He walked outside and started the car before returning to make his coffee, his final morning ritual. My mom says she woke at 8:00 a.m. for her own morning routine and was shocked to find him sleeping on the couch in his winter coat, the car still running outside and the coffeepot full of black tar. That's when the tests began. That's when he stopped working. It was the first time in his life he did not have a job. Even on his days off, he had filled empty afternoons with home projects: replacing the rust-colored wallpaper with fresh pastel prints, emptying the gutters outside, painting the front fence a brighter white.

The section on professional experience is hard to write.

"While you worked as a spray painter at the factory in Franklin, what exactly did you paint?" I ask him.

"Everything."

"Everything?"

"Yeah."

He is wearing the navy blue Foxwoods Casino T-shirt and gray sweatpants he has worn all day even though it is Thanksgiving. He crosses his thin, freckled arms, which now look like those of an old man.

"Be specific," I say. "The more specific, the better." I sound like an English teacher with her student during a one-on-one conference.

He scratches his upper arm and says, "Mostly computer parts, sometimes hospital equipment, you know, like those X-ray machines." He looks down at his slippers.

I can practically feel the cold CT scan room. Chemotherapy. Radiation. A port that had to be surgically installed above his heart so his veins could access the medicine while I held my father's hand for the first time since I was a child.

Yes, I know.

"Sometimes missiles, too."

"I'm sorry?"

"Yeah, but we were not supposed to say anything, because, you know . . ." He tilts his head in the general direction of Iraq.

"Right."

WHEN I AM DONE typing his résumé, I take the flash drive and insert it into the back of my parents' desktop computer in the living room. My mom is still talking on the phone. Long distance I suspect, because the tone of her voice has a slightly higher, more polite pitch.

The document will not open.

"What's the matter?" my father asks.

MY PARENTS BOUGHT THEIR first computer just a few months ago. My mother asked repeatedly, and I didn't help. Eventually my cousin Monica went with them to Best Buy. Monica sells yard sale items on eBay, so my mom figured she knew about *computadoras*.

"This computer doesn't have Microsoft Word, so it won't open the document," I said.

"Why does it not have it? I ordered the package deal!" My mother yell-whispers with her hand covering the phone receiver.

It's not my fault. Maybe I should've helped her order the computer. What if this doesn't work? Maybe it will work. Please work. Why do I feel guilty? This familiar emotion is stuck in my throat. I should be a better daughter. What's my problem? I am conveniently forgetting all the times my mother has hemmed my pants and skirts, the countless trips my father has taken to the mechanic on my behalf, the dozens of times both of them have driven me to the airport, attended my readings, and fed me. All this aside from having raised me in a country that wasn't their homeland and in a language that wasn't their own and, even if they didn't understand them, mostly supporting my passions for travel and writing.

"How am I supposed to know!" I whine.

My mother hangs up and calls me a *malcriada*. My father and I hover over the computer.

"Maybe you should turn it off and then on again," she says. She is still wearing her apron, having spent the better part of the day working for a wealthy family so they could enjoy their Thanksgiving dinner without being bothered to do the dishes.

"That's not going to help. The problem is you didn't order Microsoft Office, so it can't open the document," I say without looking at her.

"Well," my mother mocks, "*you* did not help us."

I SEE THE PANIC in my father's eyes. He had a similar look in his eyes when he told me it was lymphoma. It is a look I'm not used to seeing from him, one that reveals his vulnerability. I remember printing out all the information I could about it that night and the next day handing him a packet of wordy articles and black-and-white charts and diagrams. He glanced at them and stuffed them in the drawer of the hospital bedside table next to *People en Español*.

It's almost midnight. The refrigerator hums down the hall. I feel like a failure.

"Alright, look. Why don't I connect the printer to my laptop and I can just print the résumé from here?"

My mom claps. She says, "Para todo hay una solución." It's her favorite saying: For everything there is a solution.

During the next forty seconds I feel as if I am disconnecting a bomb. I need to install the printer software in my laptop, restart the computer, and plug the correct cables into their specific slots, while my father stands so close that his wheezing is distracting me. He goes to the kitchen and returns with a damp rag and a flashlight. He wipes down the desktop monitor and printer, straightens up the surrounding nest of pens and scraps of paper. Then he turns on the flashlight and shines it over my laptop, as if this will help speed up the process.

MY MOTHER PRESSES THE redial button on the cordless phone and props a pillow behind her head on the black leather couch while my father and I stare at the printer that is making sounds like it is hungry. It spits out a half-starved document. We stare at the illuminated laptop screen, the printer, and finally his résumé, his life's work described on one page that until tonight, he couldn't even hold in his hands.

LATER WHILE DRIVING BACK to my apartment on the flat, dark strip of road that is the Massachusetts Turnpike, I don't turn on the radio. I reflect on what is not on my father's résumé, what is in the white space outside the education, professional experience, skills categories, and how it is the richness of this white space that I want to explore. Years later, after we celebrate his remission with mariachis at dinner at a Mexican restaurant, after he has been feeling better for dozens of months filled with decent-paying odd jobs (but no temp work), and after he has completed a computer course at the local vocational high school, he remains a mystery to me. I might never be done wandering the white space of his résumé or stop seeking answers about his life, and this is, in part, why I want to go to Guatemala. Maybe then I will feel closer to the little boy who, on his way home from school one afternoon, stopped to stand on his horse while reaching for the ripe mango hanging from the branches above.

PART II
GUATEMALA

THE FIRST DAY

"**I**'M GOING TO GUATEMALA," I announced to my parents on Thanksgiving. Though I was twenty-eight years old and my passport bore stamps from five continents, a veil of me seeking their approval still laced my words.

Nothing.

"For six months," I added before stuffing a toasted roll in my mouth.

Still, not a word.

I decided to wait until we scooped seconds of turkey and gravy onto our plates to inform them that I had also quit my job—the one with superb benefits. They didn't need to know that I broke into my savings account to fund this trip, at least not until after the pumpkin pie. In our family, such an act would be equivalent to getting pregnant and not knowing the father.

"You gonna get killed," Dad said plainly. He chewed and stared at the wall.

"Go somewhere else," Mom piggybacked. "Italy?"

Their comments did not surprise me. They are from the very place I seek to live. Both left Guatemala in 1970 to flee rising political tensions and to pursue economic opportunities in the United States. Aside from vacations, neither returned permanently.

I ARRIVED IN GUATEMALA City on a Tuesday night. As I pushed my swollen luggage on a cart, I spotted Dad waving his arm behind the yellow gates. I grinned like I was four years old and it was bring-your-parent-to-preschool day. We hugged, but then it was right to business. How was the flight? Your mother called. Be careful here. Watch the taxi. Did you hide your money in different places?

"Yes, OK, yes, sir!"

He didn't laugh. "Stop speaking English," he snapped, ushering me through the crowd like I was a celebrity. Dad's brother, my tío, pulled up to the curb in his red Honda. My shirt clung to my sweaty back as we lifted my suitcases into the trunk.

When my father suggested meeting me in Guatemala (read: he gripped a round-trip ticket in his calloused hand), I was offended. What would my inner feminist say? A nearly thirty-year-old, college-educated woman's father treating her like a toddler? When that cloud of thought passed, I remembered: I love my father. This journey was a "roots trip," so why wouldn't I want to bring the root with me? At least for the first week. My primary intentions for traveling to Guatemala included to write, to finally correct my Spanish grammar, to write some more, to travel, to write more and more. Unfortunately, I left my laptop's power cord back in Massachusetts, amid the abandoned Balance bars I could not stuff in my suitcase, despite having sat on it half a dozen times. I decided I would go with the flow. My needs in Guatemala were already so much more basic: food, shelter, clean drinking water, bath. Perhaps it was like this in Boston too, but I had skewed vision.

We arrived in Villanueva, a gated community on the fringes of the capital, and Tío parked the car. I looked up to see that each coral-colored casita mirrored its neighbors. Tía greeted me in whispers and handed me a glass of orange juice and *pan dulce* with a block of mystery cheese. I thanked her, carried the food to my room, and plummeted onto the rollout cot. It felt like I had only been asleep for five minutes, but at nine the next morning, Dad knocked on my door.

"Listen—"

"Well, good morning to you too," I said, wiping my eyes.

"This is very important," he ignored me.

When my eyes adjusted to the million-watt bulb of a sun spilling through the windows, I took inventory of his outfit. At home he wears faded T-shirts and Lee jeans he has owned since the nineties. Here, a button-down collar, short-sleeve checkered shirt, khaki pants, and a belt.

"Yeees?"

"When you go to take a shower, whatever you do, don't touch the top wires. You can get electrocuted." He paused. "Yes, your tío almost died yesterday."

"Say what?"

"And come down for breakfast soon. They eat around 9:00 or 9:30 here." He pivoted. "Oh—" he added like I was in trouble. "That Pert Plus in there," he pushed his lips toward the bathroom, "that's mine. You can use it. It's two-in-one."

When I came down for breakfast, I immediately felt under inspection. The grammar errors in my Spanish, my too-American clothes, the way I didn't offer to pour Dad more coffee when I got more for myself, the books I carried around with me (¿Qué es *Lonely Planet?*), if I tried to read outside (¡Que creída! separating herself from the group) or inside (The light is no good, you're going to ruin your eyes). It was endless. At least Tía spared me any boyfriend questions. I should have knocked on wood because soon the telephone rang with calls—and boyfriend questions—from relatives in the capital. I explained to one aunt that these six months were not about those kinds of goals. She paused before nervously adding, "You have time."

Now that we had fried eggs, frijoles, tortillas, and coffee in our stomachs, the wide-open hours awaited. I had highlighted museums in my guidebook and circled restaurants and markets and was eager to breathe in every scent and sight in between. So I was surprised when Dad said our first stop would be the tailor. He needed to pick up a pair of pants.

In the tailor storefront, a wrinkly short guy with a silver tooth chatted us up. The woman sitting beside him on the couch asked where in the United States we were from. How did she—"Boston," Dad replied. She asked what part. "Jamaica Plain," he said. She asked what street. Soon they were talking about the Cubans and the Jews "up there" and how small the world is, how it has changed. We walked to a nearby market afterward, and two steps before the entrance, Tía reminded me, "Don't talk. They'll raise the prices if they hear your accent." So I only mouthed *Oh my God* at the sight of elderly *indígenas* in traditional textiles, kneeling on stacks of newspapers beside their fruit stands, folding spices in dried plantain leaves, all while gossiping into their cell phones. We bought some fruit and vegetables I recognized—cantaloupe and coconuts—and some I didn't—*zapotes* and *güisquils*. Later, on our way back, Dad pointed out a pair of young mothers pushing strollers with older, heavier, darker "nannies" taking smaller steps behind.

"You see," Dad said, "here, when you have a little money, you hire someone. You know, to help." It's like that everywhere, I wanted to say, but was realizing more and more that he wanted to be the one to explain things, and me to listen.

The next few days swirled with bright moments: Dad meticulously thumbing my traveler's checks as if I had never stepped foot in a bank before; visiting poor relatives who offered us soda and saltines and asked us to hold their babies to bring them good luck; meeting rich relatives who made it a point of impressing us with meals containing pricey varieties of meat and who boasted spiky hairdos complete with red highlights and side parts. We listened to stories. One tío shared how he was recently held up at gunpoint at a traffic light and had his new motorcycle stolen. Another tía explained her job in the baby garden. The what? "Sí, sí," she explained, as she bobbed a baby on her knee. "We take care of infants who are put up for adoption while the paperwork is settled in the other countries. Sometimes we have them for nine months, or eleven." Ah, yes, I remembered that one in one hundred babies born in Guatemala are adopted by families in the United States and that Guatemalan women are often coerced into doing so. Tía ordered one of her children to fetch a photo album. I nodded at the glossy photos of this baby's "parents" in Ohio and his new house in the vanilla suburbs. His big brother, however, was also Guatemalan. "Por lo menos," she said, pointing to the toddler in the picture. At least this baby would have one relative who shared his heritage.

In the evenings, we watched television and stayed up talking with our hosts. Dad talked more than usual. I loved hearing stories from his childhood—riding horseback with his mother to run long errands, how he broke his arm falling from a tree his five brothers dared him to climb, how their grandmother would rub coffee and spider webs into their wounds. "Spider webs are full of antibiotics," he clarified, anticipating my question.

Then came the time for our long-awaited drive to Xela, the nickname for Quetzaltenango. It was a part of the country neither of my parents had ever visited, and now it would be my home for the next several months. My plan was to study at a language school named Proyecto Lingüístico Quetzalteco and live with a host family for one month before writing full-time. For my parents, while growing up poor, the luxuries of travel within a country the size of Louisiana was just that: a luxury. I knew this was a special drive, the kind that I would look back on for years, decades, and maybe tell my own children about someday. The plan was for Dad to drive me to Xela before returning to Guatemala City and eventually back to Boston.

We drove in one direction: west. Having slept only one hour the night before due to a merciless mosquito, I fought my drooping eyelids all the way through the states of Escuintla, Mazatenango, each of the small pueblos, past the little boys and old men selling pineapple chunks, mangos, and coconuts with straws poking out. Huge trucks growled past, some carrying bundles of sugar cane that flicked off and looked like branches in the New England autumn. We passed a car accident—a blue truck strewn on the side of the road. I caught a glance of a body, its limbs awkwardly stretched out on the black turf. Shiny blood. Dad immediately covered my eyes with his right hand and continued to steer with his left. "Don't look! Don't eh-even look." I squinted underneath this blindfold, the palm of his hand.

We drove until the sun stood directly above us, until it folded behind us. At one point we literally drove through a cloud. "The mountains are near," he said. Yes, I could see, but more, I could feel the gargantuan stature and spirit of the highlands emerge with each kilometer. I wanted to press pause, to live this over and over again. The closer we got to our destination, the more I ached for my own childhood memories of Guatemala. Playing *avion* (the Guatemalan version of hopscotch) with my cousins in dirt alleyways, building castles on the dark purple sand beaches on the Pacific, eating frozen choco-bananas in the open-aired courtyards while our mothers prepared a potful of sweet corn drink (*atol de elote*) and *mixtas*, basically hot dogs on top of torti- llas instead of buns. But then a storefront yanked me back to my American youth: Domino's Pizza.

"You wanna stop?" he asked.

After a week of frijoles and tortillas, mozzarella cheese sud- denly sounded appealing. I nodded.

Upon returning from the bathroom, I saw Dad sitting at a round table, his belt high up on his waist, his white socks peeking out of his black Payless shoes. His shoulders hunched, he held the receipt in his hand and bit his lower lip the way my *abuelita* did. I wanted to cry and laugh and hug him and go home. Back to our old house, back to my pink Huffy bike he taught me to ride on the field at Walsh Middle School, back to the smell of spring at five o'clock in summer, back to a comfort I had forgotten, one I yearned for in this moment.

We ate greasy pizza. Got lost in Quetzaltenango for an hour. The narrow cobblestone streets and one-way signs didn't help. Eventually, we found the school. Dad rented a room at a nearby hostel. I lent him my flip-flops for the night because the communal shower was far from his room. I would stay with my host family. We were both relieved when they greeted us. A young woman in a wool sweater and jeans introduced herself and her four-year-old daughter, who cheerfully pushed around a play stroller and doll. The little girl was nonstop chatter, and she kept touching my arm and hands and ducking her head to the side while making funny faces. We learned that I would have to pass through the garage, living room, kitchen, stairs, and two brothers' bedrooms in order to reach the bathroom. Dad had *Hell no* written all over his face, especially because one brother had spiked gelled hair and a tattoo. In Dad's eyes, hair gel + tattoo = bad guy. To be more specific, a gang member.

In need of a distraction, I suggested we walk to the *parque central*. A massive pre–Semana Santa (Holy Week) processional complete with incense and chanting derailed us for an hour. We almost lost each other amid the young couples with hands tucked in one another's back jean pockets, families of four crawling like amoebas beneath fuzzy blankets, and tourists with gaping mouths and stringy hair. The floats, which were carried by men and teenage boys, consisted of saint statues displayed on beds of flower petals or maroon fabrics. They swayed in a zigzag pattern up the narrow streets and circled the park where market vendors sold plastic rosaries and fried donut balls. Dad bought plastic sandwich bags full of sticky, sweet candies made of condensed milk, coconut, almonds, marzipan, and his favorite: sesame seeds. I heard foreign languages—German, French, and one I could not identify. "They're speaking K'iche'," Dad pointed a crispy candy in the air.

The farther away we walked from the *centro*, the darker the streets became, the less swooshing of sandals on the uneven concrete sidewalks. And soon, not a sound. Soon, not a shade other than dark. We were lost. After walking past the same stone archway three times, we finally saw a gringa. Fortunately, she redirected us, but not before Dad asked her how safe she felt walking alone at night. "I don't," she said. "Actually, my friends just walked me halfway but I usually never walk alone late at night. Really, I'd say, especially for women." I tried to make eyes at her, like no, no, please stop elaborating. She didn't. "Sometimes there are robberies, and for the women," she looked at me, "rapes." OK! Thanks, chica. Dad's anxiety hit record proportions. His cheekbones in the moonlight gleamed like stones. The girl left. Eventually we found our bearings. He walked me home and said, "I don't know why you get yourself in these situations. You could have practiced your Spanish in the U.S."

All I could say was "Well . . ." He had a point, albeit a moot one. I was already in Guatemala, and there was no way I was returning to Boston. That much I knew.

In the morning, after I clicked shut the white-painted iron gate of my homestay, there stood my father in his striped sweater and jeans. Children in school uniforms trotted past him, with their young mothers trailing behind. He looked like he had been standing guard there on that street corner all night. Up until then, we were a traveling team. When I realized he would be leaving for good in a couple of hours, it was like a splinter sliced me in half. I was one thought away from choking-crying. "Let's go to the school," I said.

The school coordinator welcomed us in Spanish, and we took our seats in plastic chairs arranged in a semicircle. She led the orientation, answering all questions (most of which had to do with money and medicine and the internet) before giving a brief history of Guatemala. During the break, we met more instructors and sipped our coffee. I ate three pieces of *pan dulce* in a row. The cry was back, clotting my throat, strangling my vocal chords. I curled my toes to distract myself. My father would be heading out soon.

"OK," he said in the way he says it, o-kay. My face felt purple. I wished I were anyone or anything else: the manzanilla tea in the tall aluminum pot, the *profesora*'s hair scrunchie, the silver spider on the wall. "Well," I managed to say, "let me walk you out."

The sun in the courtyard touched my face. I heard maestros gather their students and begin one-on-one lessons. All this, until my stoicism finally crumbled. Some teachers looked my way. I didn't care. Yes, I'm twenty-eight years old and my father is dropping me off at school and it's the first day and I don't want him to leave and I am crying.

"Come on," he patted my shoulder. "It'll be OK. You'll get used to it."

"I'm OK!" I bawled. "It's you."

"What?" His eyes glassed behind his wiry frames.

There was so much I wanted to say to him. How I was sorry that I originally thought he had hijacked my trip; how I was sorry that I was so blinded. Of course he wanted to go on this journey too; of course he wanted to go with me. I didn't realize—all this time, in all my preparation—that traveling to Guatemala would have been incomplete without him.

"I know," he said, even though I had not said a thing.

So there we were. My dad. Me. We. There was nothing else to say or do. So we hugged. So we held on. So tight. Until we didn't.

GUATEMALA NOTEBOOKS: LITTLE BLACK NOTEBOOK

- Angosto = narrow. Ancho = wide.
- Empty = vacio.
- Full = lleno.

- El area
- El mapa
- El systema
- Campesinos
- Indígena
- Gente pobre, poor people

- 357 aldeas in the whole country

- verbs:
- -ar
- -er
- -ir

- Natural Medicine
- Boiled celery = drink juice left behind, helps stomach ache
- Raw red pepper with lime = for anxiety
- Plátanos with skin on, cook in hot water = the juice is really good for the brain, studying
- Eucalyptus leaves = inhale vapor, opens up lungs, cures sore throat, swollen lymph nodes

- "Art shows us that life resists us but we're still beautiful."

- "I know it's a good writer when they write a miserable world, and yet, I still want to be in that world."

- 1 Papaya = 8 Quetzales
- 1 dozen bananas = 7 Q
- 1 pineapple = 7 Q

- How to cook güisquil. If ripe, peel first. If not ripe, peel later.

THE MOUNTAIN

WOKE EARLY. TRAVELED LIGHT. I didn't want to disappoint. Not the others making the trip today. Not myself. Not my writing. This was why I was here, after all: to collect the stories. To do research for my novel. To live and breathe *like a real writer*. Or at least what I thought a *real writer* did. And, I was curious about the green-uniformed guerrilla life on the mountain. So I agreed to meet at Café RED at 5:30 a.m. I showered, brushed my teeth, and layered on the clothes: running pants, leggings, thick socks, sports bra, tank top, long-sleeve shirt, zip-up jacket, black coat. Yes, I wore eyeliner; I didn't want to look dead. I knocked on the thick black doors of Café RED. No answer. A part of me wished that maybe the whole thing had been canceled for some reason, and oh no, sorry, we have to reschedule. No problem. I'll just go back to sleep. But no such luck. A short guy in the gray sweatshirt answered the door. Well, first he opened the little secret screen where his face poked out from behind the web of metal. We looked at each other. He opened the door. He didn't say anything about my being late. The moon was bright behind me, above the dusty streets. Maybe a street lamp or two. I'm so sorry to be late. Why am I always late? I don't want him to think I'm disrespectful. Was I holding everyone up? What's wrong with me? Behind me on the street, two strangers. A father and son, a wagon loaded with bags and covered with a tarp. The little boy wore a wool hat. He was awake and happy, talking to his papa. Don't worry, says the guy at the door, the *chapin*, in the gray sweatshirt. The truck isn't here yet. So we sit at a table in Café RED, and I put some napkins in my pockets. Just in case, maybe for later. You never know. We wait. Then, a knock. Our ride. The short guy opens the door. Hello, hello, we say to Israel, who will drive us. We climb into the truck. We sit in the backseat, small as a shoebox. We're on our way to a mountain I can't name.

THE SKY LIGHTENS. WE pick up Leslie and a dude I recognize but don't know for sure. Is that bad? We wait. We wait and wait. Then we're off again. Leslie, you look beautiful, like sultry. The shorty in the sweatshirt laughs. I wonder if he knows what I said. I give him a peanut butter and jelly sandwich on whole wheat bread. I brought four. Somewhere along the road we pick up a guy named Gerardo. He climbs in the back of the truck. He says, "I was going to go back home. I thought you guys had forgotten about me." No, we're just late. On *chapin* time, not on gringo time. Then we're off again. Pushing past the farthest point I've gone in Xela. We're headed to San Marcos according to the signs. In San Martín, we pull over. That is where we pick up César. He is all smiles, and it's not even seven in the morning. He wears his plaid scarf that reminds me of Burberry. He wears fake black and white Pumas. "¿Qué onda?" He shakes every man's hand and gives the women hugs. Me, I'm one of the women. But I feel like a guy, like a compadre, I mean a *compañero*. He is white teeth and hands in his pockets. A few weeks ago I had met César at Café RED in Xela. A

Guatemalan American named Willie founded the café to give jobs to those recently deported from the United States and to those who are former guerrillas. The place offers them community and gives them purpose. César is a waiter there, an ex-guerrilla. We talked frequently. One day I interviewed him for several hours. He told me about the ways they hid rifles and machetes inside ovens and washing machines and loaded them onto trucks to be distributed around the country. Basically, he talked and I listened. We drank strong coffee. One day he invites me to visit the campground on a mountain in San Marcos where he spent years of his life, working as a soldier in Guatemala's thirty-six-year-long civil war. Of course, I say yes. Great, César says. He then hands me a tattered notebook with a red Ferrari on the cover. I open it. Inside are pages upon pages of his memories from the war, from the camp, and his beloved country. He asks me if I can help him share his story. Of course, I say. This is what I came to Guatemala for. This is a story I want to tell. I came to bear witness, and a witness is literally handing me his story.

SO HERE WE ARE. I buy 10 Q of pan dulce at a nearby *panadería* and toss the black plastic bag in the back of the truck. Hands pick out one, two pieces. We warm up with the sugar of the voyage. We're here together. There's only going forward. No back button on this day, on this experience. César looks happier than I've ever seen him to be. We leave. We stop again, after only ten minutes. What now? Someone else to jump in the back of the truck? No. César leads us to a cliff. Look out. That's where we're going. That's something Victoria, that's San this. I nod and feel grateful for the part of me that says yes to stuff like this. My father would probably kill me if he knew where I was, heading into the jungle with people I only met a few weeks ago, and mostly men. We take photos of the blurry brown hills in the distance and squint at the rising sun and there are tears from the cold collecting on the sides of my eyes and streaming sideways. Back in the truck. The radio station plays some Spanish version of Christmas songs and then suddenly Maná or Lady Gaga. We drive around curves, and I'm so thankful I've moved to the front seat. A plastic cross dangles east and west as we move fast over speed bumps that have no yellow line advertising their height. Israel, our *compa*, our driver, just pushes along, switching the radio station every seven seconds. We are moving through the fog, the morning, opening the screen to the day.

WE ARRIVE. I DON'T know how long it took. I was concentrating on not throwing up, and besides all that, I was staring out the window. So much to see. The chubby little boys, brothers in matching tan tracksuits, munching on Tortrix chips. The women balancing the country on their heads—red buckets, baskets, pineapples, tortillas, blankets, plastic combs, bananas. All kinds of bananas. Little ones. Orange ones. Green ones. Big, fat bruised ones. I wish I were a better writer, journalist, researcher. If I were a man, I'd be on this mountain with a photographer from *Virginia Quarterly Review* or *Newsweek* or both. But at least I'm here. At least I will write something. In the small town's "main street" (with three

wandering chickens and two *tiendas*), we climbed out of the truck
and stretched our legs in the sun. The temperature changed dras-
tically, from the sun to the shade, from 8:00 a.m. to 9:00 a.m.,
from a ten-minute drive up or down the incline. I wore black,
like a ninja. César brought his water canteen from the war. Green
like Private Benjamin. Gerardo even had the same backpack he
used during the war. It was faded, had several pockets, and still
worked—still held his stack of warm tortillas wrapped in a purple
cloth, a can of Ducal black beans, French bread, and water. In his
hand, a machete. I wanted to see what it felt like, so I held it in both
hands. Then one hand. It weighed as much as I thought a machete
might. I tried to cut a stem off a tree. Fail. I tried again. Fail! César
was laughing in the back; he laughed at almost everything I said
and did. When I pointed at the green leaves and someone said
those were frijoles, and I said, Ducal? He laughed when I panted
up the final hill and yelled, Hallelujah! He laughed when I asked
if he'd left love notes inside the tree—years and initials had been
marked with a knife above the tree's belly button. I stabbed the
machete into the soft ground; it reached my knee in height. I
wasn't graceful with it. It didn't know me.

I CAME TO GUATEMALA with empty journals and notebooks and with
a yearning so big that it often paralyzed me when I actually sat
down to write. So I'd go on Hulu. I know. I felt pathetic, sitting at
a table in the courtyard of my hostel, wanting so badly to write-
write-write, but then getting up for more coffee or deciding I
needed to do laundry at 10 a.m. The pressure to write came from

me. I felt I needed to set characters in capital-*H* History and to say *something*. Like, it was the least I could do as someone born to Guatemalan parents in the United States. Carry the stories forward. Never forget. The hike up the mountain felt like an opportunity. So we began. Up, up, down, down. There was no rhyme or reason to the valley. We passed simple homes with no electricity. Dogs barking and waving their tails. A toddler riding a plastic bicycle, his brother pushing him up the hill. The giggles echoing long after we passed. Israel climbed trees with little effort and snapped pictures with his red digital camera, sometimes taking short films. He was planning to just drop us off and then pick us up later. That is why he was the only one wearing dress shoes, khaki pants, and a golf shirt. Yet he was climbing all over the mountain and helping us reach for roots and tree trunks and branches as if he were an expert, a mountain guide. César laughed at that too. The sun was strong. We peeled layers. Warmed up to the idea of the darkness ahead. The irony: the jungle is all shade once you're inside. Like a cave with a giant green cover. César and Gerardo led us through the "paths" that I didn't see, ones that resembled a screen saver. I wasn't feeling scared in the physical sense. I felt in shape-enough, and I felt motivated. I thought about Joan Didion. How did she have the guts to trail through El Salvador *during* the war? I'm practically going on a tourist excursion. Or maybe, I am a messenger, as Caroline Myss describes in *Sacred Contracts*. Can I do it? I'm grown! But most days I feel like I'm eleven. I think maybe I need to drink more coffee. Stop being so dreamy. I worry about stuff sometimes, like Roth IRAs and what Suze Orman would say about dipping into my savings account to fund this trip. And then

I watch César stand in the first camp—what was really a twenty-square-foot flat patch of mountain—and talk about his days on the mountain. How they had about one hundred people altogether at one point, how everyone slept at different times in order to have guards at various posts on the mountain. They carried everything they needed on their backs. I think of Tim O'Brien.

IT'S BARELY 9:00 A.M., but it feels like 2:00 p.m. We climb. Barking dogs scare the shit out of me. I breathe like I was taught in yoga class in Brookline, Massachusetts, by tall Mark, who paced the room while holding a Starbucks cup. We keep climbing. I'm sweating, but it's the good kind of sweat, the kind that makes you feel alive in the world. The air is so fresh in my lungs, I want to cry. No diesel for many kilometers. I hear the water before I see the river. Streams in the distance. A thin black hose appears now and then, what carries the fresh mountain water to the pueblos at the bottom. A teenage boy, mustache and all, wearing knee-high rubber boots and an Abercrombie hat, carries empty white mesh bags in one hand and a machete in the other. He walks with us for part of the time, then he follows other trails that my eyes are blind to. "Have a good day," he tells us. "You too," we say. We keep going. The group, nine of us in total, move at different paces. I want to ask César follow-up questions to the many conversations we have had. What does the white hand signify again? What were the nightly reflection meetings like? Did you miss your mother on Christmas? But then I also am searching for a napkin to wipe my nose. It's all a balance. I march. We walk along the winding path, no more than two feet's width at most points, and I try not to look down, to think about what would happen if I fell, slid, plummeted to the bottom. I just look at my feet and walk with my hands in front of me like I'm reaching for the bathroom in the middle of the night. We follow César and Gerardo as they jump down the side of the mountain, machetes in hand, their feet practically floating along the lush earth. Leaves the size of humans. Soil soft as cotton. The shades of green and the smells and the bird sounds and the light and the endless kinds of healing and poisonous plants—my mind swirls. I am humbled. Ow! A leaf prickles my hand. I reach for a tree and its mossy green texture does nothing to help me with my grip as I climb down the mountain. Another time I reach for a branch and its million thorns jolt me into finding another way not to fall. I used my four limbs. I move my neck and head sideways and up and under. I grab roots and use them like ropes to make my way up and down the earth. At one point I say aloud, "It smells like Home Depot."

LESLIE HAD A HARD time with some of the hike. She slid a lot and looked like she was about to surrender fully, but then Israel would help her. I felt for her. I was hitting a breaking point too. Not as bad, but definitely beginning to wonder how lost we were. Many men never want to admit they are lost, much less stop for directions. But here, on the mountain, who would they ask anyway? Gerardo couldn't remember where the trail was that led to the second camp. His memories were probably fogging his vision. César's smile and *no-hay-problema* way is comforting, but even that only goes so far. Dirt under my nails. Dirt in my sneakers. Israel made us "a bridge" over the water by lifting heavy rocks and positioning them in strategic parts of the river so we could step on them and not have to soak our feet. How did he know to do that? I wondered if it wasn't much like writing. How did I know how to write? What to write? You just put one rock in front of the other. Make bridges on the page. Here, deep in the jungle, hungry and tired and thirsty, I was apparently getting philosophical too. But it was true. Eventually we reach the second camp. My stomach is rumbling, but it sounds like an outside sound. Like one that belongs to the forest, not to me. It mixes in with the blackbirds and the stream and the rustling of leaves as we move about. The snapping of pictures from various cameras. We drop our packs. This is it? I'm thinking. Again, the camp is no bigger than a studio apartment. No bigger than a doctor's waiting room. Mosquitoes EVERYWHERE. Until then we'd been moving steadily, but now, they gnawed and feasted on us like we were game. It was distracting to say the least. At one point I ducked my head underneath my navy blue shirt and just listened to Gerardo and César give their talks. I couldn't breathe without a mosquito getting sucked up my nostril or landing on my tongue. We sat together, close, even though there was clearly room to spread out. We each pulled out food from our packs, if we had them, and placed items in the center of the circle. Like an offering. Like, okay, this is what I bring to the collective. None of this, Well, I'll trade you half my pb and j for a piece of your *tamalito*. No! It was a feast for all: paches, hardboiled eggs, tortillas, pan, frijoles, chicken in pulled strings in a Tupperware container from César's wife. Pineapple chunks

I'd cut up at 5:00 a.m. and placed in a Xelac yogurt container. We ate. We didn't talk much. Just dipped pieces of tortillas in the *recado* and then the Ducal container. I brought salt. Packed it in an old orange and white prescription bottle.

EVERYONE SHARED. EVERYONE ATE. The way of the mountain is sort of the way of the whole country. Guatemalans give everything they can, but they don't waste anything either. Like at the school supply store, they sell one sheet of wrapping paper at a time. Different patterns, colors, everything, but it's one square sheet, at one quetzal each. I tried to focus on César, who talked a bit about the days in the camp. Gerardo seemed a little more distant, reserved, like maybe even suspicious of our intent. Were we genuinely interested, or were we trying to get a good workout in and be voyeurs for a day? I get it. I would be the same way. But he warmed up when I told him that I loved his comments in the documentary they'd shot the last time they'd come up to the mountain. I even had my notes with me in a purple notebook I bought at Target before coming to Guatemala. César searched the perimeter of the camp and came back holding an old (empty, of course) bottle of rum and a cassette case. "See!" he announced. "We had fiestas up here. Navidades. We drank and danced. See?" He holds the bottle up in the air. The dirty cassette cover, no label. "See . . ." His voice trails to a whisper as he stares at the possessions in his hands. Proof! Someone jokes. ¡Prueba! Yes, you were here. You were here. And you are here again now.

GERARDO BROUGHT US BACK to the serious part of war. He said that once the government had announced that it would sign peace accords and that the war was essentially "over," some guys had a really hard time dealing with that. For them, this was the way of life. For them, this is all that they'd known. The war, in many cases, took their youth with it. They gave *that* up, like an offering. Once they returned to "civilization," they didn't have families, houses, jobs, or government checks waiting for them. Gerardo says he remembers one guy really struggling. "One *compa*," he said, "didn't want to turn in his gun. He couldn't do it. I picture the man crying and struggling to give up his arms." Then Gerardo explained that when Ríos Montt said something like "If you cannot catch the fish, you have to drain the sea," he meant killing these families so they couldn't support the guerrillas anymore. I thought of the families we'd passed at the foot of the mountain. Somehow, seeing them in the flesh brought a whole new meaning, made it all the more real. The way back down the mountain felt shorter. I was thirsty. A kind of thirst I knew was a fraction of the thirst from the war, but still. *One* afternoon, *one* day, I could say, I spent there. They spent years, over a decade on the mountain. At one point after lunch I saw Gerardo brushing his teeth in the river. Was it habit? Was it intentional? What happens to former guerrillas when there is no more war? He wanted to connect in such a way that we couldn't. I mean, I suppose we *could* have. But then again, it wasn't about us.

A few months later, I left Guatemala and returned to the States. I could not bear to take César's journals with me even though he wanted me to. They belonged to him. So we photocopied them at a copy center in Xela. I carried the pages with me to various writing residencies over the years, but mostly, they sat in a box with other material I'd get to someday. Whenever I "saw" him on Facebook, I felt horrible. It was a reminder of how I had failed to transcribe his journals (I tried a few times, I really did) and make something from them, a chapbook or something, in English and Spanish, that he could sell in Café RED. But I didn't do it. I never did it.

BY THE END OF the hike we were barely talking. More like muttering and gesturing and trying to stay out of one another's way. The last stretch felt like twelve hours. My throat was dry, beyond dry. Thing is, on the mountain there was water. Plenty of it. They said we should refill our water bottles in the river, but I said no way, no. "Why? It's *agua pura*. What contaminates water is people— germs, disease. But here, this . . . ," César's voice trailed off, then lifted once more, "this, is the natural thing."

GUATEMALA NOTEBOOKS:
LA VOZ POPULAR

Speaker: Maria Tulia
   Guerrilleros needed a clandestine radio. They would cover the cables and batteries with leaves and climb up the trees and hang the radio there, with antennae. Had to keep moving location so the army wouldn't find them. Sometimes they buried the radio in the ground, so no evidence.
   The radio shows aired after 8:00 p.m. so people in their homes could hear them. Had versions for rural people, too, using more common language.
   La Voz de la Gente
   Show also had a space for medical advice, e.g., women should have a beer after giving birth, etc.

1 apple = 55 calories

Book rec from Claire—*The Astonishing Power of Emotions*
   "It is not what you are *doing* that makes the difference, it is how you are *feeling* about what you are doing."

Miguel Ángel Asturias—first person in Guatemala to earn Nobel Prize in Literature

·   Jeannette Valdez
·   Cellular: 55555559
·   Casa: 55555551

List for Mom when she visits:
1.   Luna bars
2.   Coffee-mate
3.   Olive oil
4.   Ziploc bags (lots)
5.   Jhumpa Lahiri book?

LOS MONÓLOGOS
DE LA VAGINA

"MEN ARE PIGS," MY teacher Brenda said.
We were seated at a square wooden table inside Proyecto Lingüístico Quetzalteco (PLQ). It was my fourth week at the Spanish-language school in Xela. Through the tall window I could see the magenta flowers in the courtyard, their petals shivering with the occasional breeze. It felt like a cool spring day in New England, but by the looks of Brenda, we were minutes away from a blizzard. She wore a pink knit hat, white gloves, and a puffy gray coat. Her pale, thin fingers poked out of gloves missing their fingertips. I wore khakis, a T-shirt, and a Guatemalan scarf I had bought from one of the women on the street outside the school. Brenda was the fourth teacher I had studied with so far at PLQ. She had pin-straight black hair and bangs, and like me at the time, she was in her late twenties. If I was feeling the pressure to be married and have babies, I could only imagine the anxiety she felt. In Guatemala, a twenty-eight-year-old single woman was considered a spinster.

"Well, maybe they're not all pigs," Brenda added. Her eyes glazed over. I imagined her playing a reel of some memory of a previous romance. Part of me wanted to get back to the worksheet between us, the one with sentences whose blanks I had to complete using *por* or *para*. I was paying money to study Spanish after all.

Yet, another part of me wanted her to share whatever clip she was obviously lingering on as she stared out the window. Then, suddenly, she shifted her gaze toward me, as if she were seeing me for the first time. What did I look like to her? What did she make of my "traditional" Guatemalan scarf over a T-shirt I probably paid forty dollars for back in Boston? By then, all of the teachers at the school knew about me, Jenny, the one from *los Estados*, the one who is Guatemalan and speaks Spanish but wants to be *more* Guatemalan and speak *better* Spanish, yes, that one.

In the beginning of my stay here, though, no one really knew what to make of me. I was here to study Spanish, write a novel, and learn about Guatemalan history. Still, no one knew how to *see* me. The first evening my host mother, Blanca, picked me up from the language school, and we walked to her house where I would live for several weeks; night was on the horizon and quickly swallowing the city avenues. The city of Xela was not exactly known for its streetlights. Night draped over us and, with it, took the familiar lady selling *atole de elote* on the street corner, the school supply store across the street, and the yellow wall that served as a friendly reminder to walk this way, the school will be just down the street on the right. None of that helped me then, and even though I was with Blanca, I still carried homesickness behind my heart. These were not my streets. These were not my people. What if I was making a big mistake by thinking I could actually live in Guatemala? Write a novel?

Blanca abruptly stopped, turned around. "Forgive me for asking this question, but . . ."

A car's headlights beamed in our direction, magnifying the moment. What did she want to ask me? And why couldn't the question wait until we arrived at the house, after I showered and changed and wrote in my journal and ate something?

She cleared her throat. "If you're Guatemalan and you already speak Spanish, and your parents and family are Guatemalan, then what are you doing here?"

And there it was. This was the question, the axis on which my entire trip spun.

I sighed and said something like, "Oh, I just want to improve my Spanish, and I'm working on a book." She squinted at me, a genuine and curious expression all over her face, as if my response only ignited more questions. But those would wait.

"Bueno," she said. "You are welcome here."

"Thank you," I said and followed her home.

AT PLQ I HAD heard the teachers wanted to work with me, not so much because I was Guatemalan but because they could speak Spanish the whole time and not have to suffer through painful pronunciation lessons with foreigners. Sometimes during the morning coffee break, teachers would come up to me and stroke my arms. They would ask, "Who are you working with next week, Jenny?" All the teachers at PLQ were magnificent in their own way, but I had been waiting to work with Brenda because she was the youngest. I didn't think she liked me very much. I got the feeling that she thought I was spoiled. I put my suspicions aside, though, because I wanted to learn more about the modern Guatemalan woman. My *primas* in the capital had given me glimpses, but I could tell they were limited in what they could share. Their parents, my aunts and uncles, kept them on tight, invisible leashes. God forbid they share something too scandalous, too honest, and I would report back to my mother and relatives in Massachusetts.

"This is the thing," Brenda said, like I'd asked her a question and wasn't just sitting there clicking my pen. "The pool of eligible men gets smaller and smaller every day." I thought of the men summoning spit from the deepest parts of their throats and hawking the globs onto the sidewalk. "Especially the more education a woman has, and especially the older she gets because she is *not* going to stand for a typical macho husband, *no way*. But then there is this tremendous societal pressure to get married, have kids. In Guatemala, there are few who go against the norm, and it's hard, but my friends and I, we do it. We don't want to change back. Do you understand?"

I thought of my cousin Flory in Guatemala City, how when she turned twenty-five her mother, my tía Emerita, started asking if there were any cute boys she'd seen at church. A couple years later when Flory was scheduled to undergo ovarian surgery, the doctor told her that if she ever wanted her own biological child, then this was her last chance. So she was artificially inseminated and gave birth to a healthy daughter. Now, into her thirties, Flory was raising her daughter as a single mother. Tía Emerita was much more freethinking with her second daughter, Cynthia. She allowed her to have a boyfriend while she was still in university. She even brought him to the house. Everyone loved this muchacho because he worked part-time at a bank.

"Yeah," I answered Brenda and adjusted my scarf that suddenly felt too tight.

Brenda still lived with her parents. She had studied at the local university in Xela and now worked as a teacher at PLQ, which attracted liberal-minded foreigners who wanted to study Spanish. Two of these students included Tiana and Shira, who were organizing the production of the popular play *The Vagina Monologues*. The play consisted of a series of short skits and in most cases monologues that dealt with various parts of, well, the vagina. Menstruation, sex, rape, domestic violence, sexual climax, female power, sex versus love, and one skit involving a young girl asking, If my vagina were a fruit, what would it be? If my vagina could talk, what would it say? That sort of thing. I had first seen the play in college. I remember witnessing a woman on stage narrate the symphonic range of female orgasms. It was amazing.

It was Tiana who asked if I would be interested in performing one of the skits.

"Me? Oh, no, no, no. I don't think I could do that. In Spanish? Which skit? Would I have to do it alone? No. I don't think so."

"Come on. It's kind of a once-in-a-lifetime opportunity. It's no big deal."

Wasn't that an oxymoron? To be on stage, talking about vaginas, and *in Spanish*?

Tiana twisted her mouth. "You could do the menstruation skit. It's less intense. And it'd be a group, like sitting in chairs in a semicircle."

This, I considered. I felt safer in a group. I would have specific lines. The audience would have several of us to focus on, not just me. And Tiana was right, it was kind of a once-in-a-lifetime opportunity to perform in *Los Monólogos de la Vagina* in Quetzaltenango, Guatemala.

"Okay," I agreed.

Three other women and I were to sit on chairs in a semicircle and read our lines from small pieces of paper if we needed to, but of course we were encouraged to memorize our lines if we could.

"Great. Trust me. You can totally do it. It's no big deal," Tiana said. "Only thing is, we need a fourth person. Do you have any ideas?"

I thought for a moment. "Maybe Blanca?"

"Your host mom?"

"Yeah. Why not? It's for Guatemalan women, isn't it? Half the women in the play are Guatemalan anyway. That's what you said."

Blanca was easy to recruit. I told her that it would be a unique opportunity to participate in a wonderfully feminist and fun activity. "Vaya pues," she said. I wasn't surprised. She told me that once, about ten years ago, she was leaving the bank in the parque central. She carried a wad of cash in her purse because she was on her way to pay the electricity bill. A man attacked her from behind and ran off with her purse. Instead of screaming for help, not that the apathetic security guards would do anything, Blanca chased the robber down the street until she caught up with him. She jumped on his back until he fell face down. She turned him around and while sitting on him, proceeded to punch him in the face until he bled from his nose. She got her purse back. Yes, I knew Blanca would be easy to recruit.

FOR THE FOLLOWING FEW days I studied Spanish with Brenda in the mornings and rehearsed the menstruation skit in the afternoons, mostly at the school, sometimes in the courtyard. The performance would take place Saturday night. Tiana and Shira instructed all of the performers to wear black and red the night of the event. Teachers of all ages (including Brenda), teenagers, and even one ten-year-old girl participated in the play. In total, there were about thirty Guatemalan and foreign women. Minutes before the performance, which took place at the cultural center beside the school—a space that Tiana, Shira, and several volunteers completely transformed to look like a set out of Broadway—we all huddled in one of the small classrooms on the second floor. I could hear the crowd buzzing downstairs. People all over Xela had been talking about the play day and night and now it was finally here. This was the first time that anything like this was being performed at the cultural center or in the city of Quetzaltenango. The line for seats was out the door, onto the street, around the corner. The tickets sold out faster than the pink vagina cookies on sale for three quetzales each. All the proceeds went to support the only women's shelter in all of Xela.

Minutes before show time, Shira led the group in a community building activity. Years later I'd learn on social media that she became a midwife in New York City and she sometimes posted photos of glossy, thick, disc-shaped placentas. She told us we were going to go around in a circle and that each one of us had to finish this sentence: "*Me llamo_____ y yo aaaamo mi vagina. Dedico esta presentación a_____ porque_____.*" (My name is_____ and I loooove my vagina. I dedicate this performance to_____ because_____.)

When it was my turn, I remember saying something like, "My name is Jenn and I loooove my vagina. I dedicate this performance to my ancestors because they would never be caught dead doing a performance like this one." Everyone laughed. It was true; Guatemalan women were traditionally taught *not* to talk about anything to do with sex, female anatomy, sexual pleasure, periods, nothing. It was private, secret, even shameful to discuss, especially in public. I was raised to believe that tampons were a creation of the Devil, okay, maybe not that dramatic, but still. My sisters and I would never admit to our mother that we used tampons, not until our twenties. At the lake in the summer we would wear oversized T-shirts on top of our bathing suits. Makeup was off-limits. Slowly, we won mini-battles—eyeliner became tolerable by senior year in high school, for example. Boyfriends? Yeah, right. Not until college, anyway, and even then, my father often ignored the "friends who were boys" that I brought home with me to Massachusetts.

My mind swirled with these memories and cultural taboos as I stood in this circle with all these women, and the abundance of female energy and power and laughter and excitement really puffed me up like a balloon. I gripped the hands of the women on my right and left, and I took in the red and black outfits, even down to the black eye shadow and red lipstick. Guatemalan women. American women. And me, a Guatemalan American woman. Always seeming to occupy that space in between, yet still part of the circle in my own way. My stomach tensed. The performance was minutes away. We made our way back downstairs and sat on chairs that had been set up on the right side of the space so we could easily step on and off the main stage. I sat beside Blanca, my host mother, and Maria Tulia, a former guerrillera and genocide survivor. The next week I would work with her. We will sit on the school rooftop, and aside from correcting some of my grammar in Spanish, she will share stories from her past, about working for La Voz Popular, the underground radio station for the guerrilla movement for which she received training in Cuba, and about her life in the revolution.

But for now, the lights flashed and the audience went wild. I could see several teenagers in the audience, spike-haired boys in tight, faded jeans and fitted white T-shirts holding hands with their dates, girls with long straight black hair and heavy eye makeup. I noticed a few mother-daughter pairs and some older women seated in a group, together. Then, the lights dimmed. On stage the first performer sat on a stool and spoke into a microphone, detailing the injustices brought against her vagina—from, yes, tampons, to the cold metal tools used by gynecologists. Everyone clapped. Some of the monologues were more serious than others, and some funny and light (Why should I shave my vagina? Hair is there for a reason). The audience cheered and cried and stood and nodded, and yes, their eyes bulged as one performer dramatically presented a range of orgasms—from an angry, low sound to a high-pitched, birdlike sound, from a brief beep to an extended moan. I thought I might float up to the night sky.

Our turn came. I was so proud of my host mom, Blanca, who, in her tight nylon pants, black T-shirt, and red scarf, performed her lines with gusto. Menstruation, rape, virginity, marriage, childbirth, and, yes, climax reached new heights this evening in Xela. I felt stitched into a time and place that would always matter, to me, to these women, to this community. Immediately after the final performance, many of the women were presented with roses and bouquets from family and friends in the audience. People took pictures. Others made plans for grabbing drinks downtown. I bought a vagina cookie. It was one of the last ones. I remember going out with others for a celebratory beer before returning home to Blanca's and falling asleep.

But I remember more one moment when I caught my teacher Brenda's eyes. Our week of studying was now done. She was seated in the row of chairs beside me as we waited our turns to perform. I still didn't think she liked me very much, that she thought I was probably spoiled and naïve. Maybe I was. But then she winked at me, and I smiled. Even though we were the same age, I felt younger, childlike compared with her, like she had done more living just by growing up here in Guatemala. It was something I could never do or be, no matter how much I studied or how many months I spent here. I thought of what she'd said earlier this week, how in her eyes the pool of eligible husbands-to-be was shrinking each day, how she thought men were pigs. Later I would learn she married a foreigner from Washington State and had a baby and moved to the States permanently. I wondered to whom she dedicated her performance that night. I wondered if she missed Xela. If she missed her parents. And I wondered if she and I were in the same circle again, holding hands and declaring our love for our vaginas, to whom we might dedicate our performances this time. Our daughters? Our sons? I would like to think that I would dedicate my performance to my younger self, to the girl who did not know where she would land or with whom but who believed in something more.

GUATEMALA NOTEBOOKS:
LIFE IN THE CAMPO

- Men earn 17 quetzales a day.

- Start/leave for work at 3 AM so wives have to wake up at 1 AM to prepare food for day.
- Rain, mud, truck often gets stuck.
- Sometimes get home at 10, 11, 12, only to turn around and do the same thing again.

VOLCÁN TAJUMULCO

WE LEFT BEFORE DAWN. We met in front of the school with our backpacks full of the very thing we could not stop talking about for most of the two-hour bus ride to San Marcos: food. We were two-dozen foreign students, two Guatemalan guides, and one bus driver. The guy with the ponytail showed off a heavy bag of pumpkin granola. His buddy brought a loaf of bread and four hotdogs wrapped in tinfoil. One German girl said that after much debate, she eventually stuffed a Nutella jar in her backpack last minute.

We arrived at the foot of Volcán Tajumulco, the highest volcano in Central America (4,220-meter peak). The Mayans often held ceremonies up there because, they believed, it was closer to God. My lungs were tight, my throat dry. Rows of pine trees and clay-colored hills spread in the distance. The sky was the color of water. Guatemalans believed that if you approached the journey with fear, if you hiked with panic about getting sick or lost, you would get sick or you might get lost. The volcano would punish you for your doubt. However, if you went in with faith, then you would be fine. The others began chugging water. Two blonde girls from Denmark helped each other adjust their packs, while another traveler applied sunscreen onto her nose and ears. I tightened my shoelaces. The hike would take about five hours, which at that altitude translated to about twenty-five hours. The driver explained, again, that the risk of sickness was great and that because of the altitude, the hike itself, and then camping overnight in the frigid temperatures, we might want to reconsider going at all. "This is the last chance to come back with me to Xela. No one will judge you," he said. He wore dark jeans and a leather jacket over a button-down shirt. A gold cross dangled from his neck.

The guides waved their arms, calling everyone in to form a circle.

The van driver, looking at me, asked again, "Are you sure you want to hike the volcano?"

Students were busy adjusting lenses on their fancy cameras, tightening ponytails, and tucking Gore-Tex T-shirts into Gore-Tex pants.

"You can still come back to Xela," the driver repeated. "No hay problema."

My feet sank down into the earth tender and brown as my skin. I shut my eyes tight and inhaled the sweet mountain air. No hay problema.

Our two guides could not have been more different. Amaro looked to weigh 110 pounds. He wore green cargo pants, a wool sweater, hiking boots, and a khaki fishing hat. He hated America. He hated Americans. Later, I would learn that he really just hated the fact that the United States government had funded the war in Guatemala for so many years, taking with it so many innocent lives. He was not on the side of the pro-capitalist army. Instead, Amaro lived as a guerrilla in the mountains, alongside his father, who had been kidnapped and tortured before escaping the army barracks one day. Now, Amaro and his father worked for Proyecto Lingüístico Quetzalteco (PLQ). His father gave lectures and personal testimonies from time to time. Amaro explained to the group, now huddled in a circle, that we must try and stay together as much as possible. "Never hike alone," he said. He would walk ahead and guide us, while Fito, the other guide, would hike at the tail end, making sure no one was left behind. We would stop three times for water and food breaks, but other than that, we would not stop until we reached the campground by sunset. "Understood?"

"Yes, sir!" I wanted to say, but he didn't look like the joking kind. He turned around and started hiking even before Fito was done translating for him. Fito wore Timberland boots, enormous wide-legged jeans, a white turtleneck, and a huge navy blue rain-coat that fell to his knees. The tents he had strapped to his back-pack were hanging at odd angles, and his cheeks were red, even though we hadn't yet started the climb. A plastic supermarket bag tied in a knot suspended from his pack. In it, I could see a few individual sized packages of Tortrix chips, one orange Fanta, and a Snickers candy bar.

So we hiked. I alternated between taking many small steps and fewer, wider ones. Neither method reduced the huffing and puffing. I squinted. I wheezed. Soon I spotted specks of red and blue bobbing packs up ahead. The Germans. I pushed harder. I vowed to never smoke again, not even when I was drunk, not even on New Year's Eve. The muscles in my legs pulsed, burned. My back ached with the pressure of the pack.

THE VIEWS FROM VOLCÁN Tajumulco made me feel like I was stand-ing inside a glass of water. Wind wrapped around me like gauze as I climbed. My chest visibly heaved. By this point we had been hiking for close to three hours. I mostly stayed by myself. Talking and hiking were like oil and water: they didn't mix. Branches crackled in spaces I could hear but could not see. Birds cawed in their secret bird language. The crunching sound of my marching feet was hypnotic, soothing. It grew louder as I hiked, and that's when I realized that someone else was marching behind me. Fito. Oh shit, I thought. I really was the last one in the group.

"What's your name?" he asked in English.

"Jennifer," I said, pausing to catch my breath from having spoken the one word.

"Jenny from the Block!" He laughed, coughed, cleared his throat, and sped up to walk in stride with me.

"Yeah. Jennifer Lopez."

"You like her?"

"Me? Oh, I guess so. Not really."

"How about Mariah Carey?"

"Yeah, I like her."

"Where you from?"

"Well, my parents are actually from here. I live in Boston though."

"Chapina?"

"Yeah." I was sure that my lungs were about to collapse at any moment. How the hell did the guerrilla soldiers run up and down hidden trails and distribute weapons and report from clandestine radios all while surviving on the goodwill of campesinos at the foot of the mountain to bring them tortillas and beans every few days? How did *Fito*? Supposedly he had lived on Tajumulco in a guerrilla camp when he was a teenager. I stared at the yellow ring around his white turtleneck. He spit out his gum. A neon green ball flung from his mouth and landed not far on the path.

"Is gum biodegradable?" I asked, like an idiot.

He winced, adjusting the straps of his backpack on his shoulders. "What?"

"Never mind."

We didn't say much after that. Every effort to speak pulled on my lungs.

Twenty minutes later we came upon the rest of the group. They were all spread out underneath the canopy of trees, feeding each other fruit and resting. Together they looked like a Victorian painting, only they weren't naked. They were dressed in Patagonia fleeces. A couple of the guys had traded their hiking boots for Teva sandals, their bare feet as white as lightbulbs.

I offered Amaro a boiled egg, which he accepted with a low *gracias* and returned to his position away from everyone else. I wondered what he was thinking as he stared out at the vast scenery below, the dips and folds of the mountains and trees and clouds like something out of a fairy tale. What did he make of these foreigners, myself included, most of whom flew down to Guatemala for a week, a month, maybe even a year, to leave and never come back? Without us, students wanting to learn Spanish in a sociopolitical school that included field trips in their weekly tuition, Amaro wouldn't have a job.

We continued up the mountain. I wasn't so sure if the sun had dipped behind a series of clouds or if it was getting later, probably a combination of both, but the blue sky had left for good. Once we finally reached the campsite, Amaro and Fito immediately began to set up a fire. It seemed everyone else was pulling out wool-knit hats and thick socks and moving behind a tree to change into long underwear. No one had told me to bring any of that. I swallowed the last drops of my water bottle.

Amaro called us over. I sat on a log across from him. A girl shared her jar of Nutella with her friends but no one else. I could see Fito eyeing it. At first, Amaro spoke generally about the world-wide battle between democracy and communism. He began by mentioning the CIA-sponsored coup in 1954, which overthrew Guatemala's democratically elected president at the time, Jacobo Árbenz Guzmán.

"Up until then, all the presidents had supported the interests of the United Fruit Company," he said. Fito translated, adding, "They're the ones who produced all the bananas and stuff like that."

"There were a few failed attempts to restore democracy. But the United States government feared the widespread communism. Guatemala's rich agreed."

"Why?" one girl innocently asked.

"Why?" Amaro repeated. He didn't sound angry, so much as genuinely perplexed. Had this girl been so sheltered her whole life not to understand that most rich people liked to remain rich, no matter what? "People in the city, wealthy people, they don't see where their tortillas come from," he said. "They don't understand what it is to live without shoes, to not know how to read, to bury baby corpses because of hunger and illness. It was Guatemala's poor that suffered the most."

The girl blinked slowly. "I know that. I meant, why did the attempts for a democratic reelection fail after the coup? Wasn't there a strong coalition of Árbenz supporters?"

"Assassinations," Amaro said. "That's why. Anyone considered a threat, that is, a leader or anyone who had any influence in town, including politicians and priests, or really anyone who appeared a leftist, was kidnapped, tortured, and often killed. Sometimes vans full of armed military or police kidnapped men and women in broad daylight. They forcefully interrogated them until they got the answers they were looking for, and if they didn't get them, then, well . . ." Amaro looked down at his feet. His laces were undone and the tongues of his boots stuck out.

Fito was having difficulty keeping up with the translating. After a while, Amaro asked us to raise our hands if we could understand most of what he was saying in Spanish. Did we still need it all translated, or could he just keep going?

He kept going. "So, by 1970, Carlos Arana rose to head of state. He was also known as the 'Butcher of Zacapa' for all the massacres that took place while he directed the counterinsurgency campaign in the late 1960s. He once said, 'If it is necessary to turn the country into a cemetery in order to pacify it, I will not hesitate to do so.'"

One guy with a brown ponytail stood up, crossed his arms, and began to pace.

"Thousands were kidnapped and murdered under the administration of Lucas García. By the time Ríos Montt came around," Amaro said, shaking his head, "we were fucked."

"Really fucked," Fito said. He tossed a branch into the fire, and it seemed to smother the flame rather than catch light.

I had heard of Ríos Montt. He oversaw Scorched Earth. He was basically a Latino Hitler responsible for the genocide of tens of thousands of innocent campesinos in the Guatemalan countryside. I thought of one of my Spanish teachers at PLQ in Xela, Maria Tulia. She had been kidnapped. She had been blindfolded and thrust into a helicopter and told she would only survive if she gave up names.

"*Entonces* the four guerrilla groups—EGP, ORPA, FAR, and PGT—formed the URNG." Amaro lifted his sweater and revealed a T-shirt with the letters URNG.

He also told us about the underground radio station that the URNG had established. They used it to communicate with each other but also to reach the people. The army could never find the radio source because it constantly moved. Amaro smiled big when he talked about the radio. "They never found us."

A few students asked questions regarding the refugees who had fled to Chiapas and Tabasco. I wanted to ask about the women. What did a woman do when she got her period? What happened if she got pregnant?

By now, night had fallen. The cold left our mouths in smoky puffs. Fito passed around a jar of honey and instructed us to eat spoonfuls of it in order to stay warm overnight.

"My father was kidnapped and tortured," Amaro said. The orange flames cast a glow on his face, his skin dark like bark, his high cheekbones and intense eyes. "My father could be anyone's father. He could be your father, sí?"

"I guess . . ." the same girl from before looked close to tears.

"I couldn't just sit there while my country suffered. I couldn't live in a country where there was no democracy. Not unless I was doing something to change it."

THAT NIGHT I WAS cold to the point of actually crying. I had forgotten to pack one of those sleeping bag pads that prevent the earth from absorbing all your body heat, or whatever. I kept thinking about Amaro's stories, especially the one about his father being kidnapped. Maybe it was my insomnia or something about being on the very volcano that so many guerrilla soldiers occupied during the war, but my imagination was on overdrive. I imagined how the Guatemalan Army raided Amaro's family's village. Soldiers slaughter the elderly first, next the women, and finally the children. The men, they torture. The strong ones are kidnapped, and the weak ones are shot in the backs of their heads. In my nightmare, Amaro stares at his father whose pupils are so dilated that Amaro can see the reflection of the volcanoes in them. Then a soldier pours gasoline and lights a match to his father. Flames devour his father's arms, legs, and torso while he slithers in the dirt and the soldiers laugh standing around him in a circle. Amaro screams. Patches of his father's skin have melted off in clumps, and his hair emits a horrible stench. When he leans closer, it's not his father's face he sees on his father's body. It's his own. Amaro wakes to his wife tugging his arm. "¡Despiertate!" she says. "Wake up. You're having another nightmare."

I was scaring myself with another person's imagined nightmare. What was wrong with me? And why had I forgotten to bring a sleeping bag pad? I didn't know it would be so cold here. Then, I heard something. A shuffling of some sort. An animal? Oh dear God, no. Next, I heard a voice. Fito. He was coughing and laughing. I crawled out of the tent and wrapped my sleeping bag around me like an oversized shawl. Fito and Amaro were smiling and smoking as they stood around the fire. I practically wept now from joy. Heat. Light. Two Guatemalan guys who could be my cousins.

"Hey, it's Jenny from the Block," Fito said. He passed me the jar of honey with a white plastic spoon sticking out of it.

"Thanks," I said.

We talked around the fire until the first streak of pink appeared in the sky. I learned that Fito had recently been deported back to Guatemala. He had been living in Corpus Christi, Texas, where as a high school senior he won "Most Likely to Win an Oscar" for his performance in the student musical *Grease*. Fito played Danny, the starring role. That is what he missed most about America he said: anyone who works hard and has talent can make it. But because Fito was deported days before his high school graduation, he never got to receive his diploma from the principal. He asked if I could help him get a copy of his high school diploma. "I know it's just a piece of paper," he said. "But it's important to me."

"I can try," I said.

Mostly Fito and I talked. Amaro squatted every now and then to feed the fire. At one point, when I bent down to tighten my laces, Amaro looked at me as if for the first time. After a brief awkward silence, we both stood up. It was then that he spoke about his family, and I spoke about my family, and Fito about his family. Finally I was able to ask Amaro my questions about women guerrillas. "If they got pregnant," he said, "they worked until they couldn't work anymore, and then someone escorted them to a midwife, usually a supporter in a nearby community." It made sense.

Then he twisted his face and in a low voice said, "Leaves."

"Hmm?"

"To answer your other question." He stared at the tall flames. "Many women used leaves."

GUATEMALA NOTEBOOKS: CHILD WORKERS

- Working child 6–12 years old.
- Un niño trabajador—many think it's a dirty kid selling stuff on the street.
- A certain kind of discrimination against them. When really this results from overall poverty, etc. Rural areas worse: lack of schools, teachers, etc.

- *Why isn't school after 6th grade mandatory?*
- [It costs $65 per year to go to middle school.]

- Xela. Kids pick rocks and break them up to make cement— a common job here.
- 8 AM–1 PM. Half day of school (like mom)
- If Ministry of Education does provide breakfast, it's only una galleta y un vaso de atol de elote—not enough.
- "Just go to school" is not that simple, must go to get clothes, shoes, uniforms, bags, supplies, food to send. We may think parents are exploiting their children, but 1,400 Q/per month is minimum wage.

LUCKY WOMAN

HAVE HEARD THE STORY many times. How, three decades after deserting my grandmother and their eight children in Guatemala, my grandfather asked for her forgiveness. I imagine her, Luisa, standing in my parents' kitchen in Massachusetts, using the side of her wrinkled hand to wipe crumbs from the counter. She tosses them into the sink, a metal box where she can make hot water run, miraculously, by turning the left handle to the right. No need for a horseback ride to the river. No need even for a horse. Here, there are cars. Here, there are wide, paved roads.

Of all the girls in the villages that dotted the southern coast of Guatemala, Luisa was the one my grandfather chose. They married in the town of Tiquisate, where they signed a document in the presence of an *alcalde*, the mayor. They lived on a farm, in a simple house that sat beside a long row of lime trees in one direction and, in the other, a dusty dirt path that led to the rest of the world. Their days: milking cows, fishing, hanging cured meat from the ceiling, making love in the country darkness. They had six boys. My father was number three. Women called Luisa lucky. Her husband was handsome and smart. When he didn't come home for days, she figured he was just smoking hand-rolled cigarettes with communists. When she learned he'd been with another woman, she forgave him. He was the only man she had ever loved. They had a seventh baby, a girl. They had no money.

They traded limes for avocados, sugar, and shoelaces. My grand-father found work at the United Fruit Company. At the end of each day he brought home bunches of bananas and powdered milk in cans whose labels were written in English. Before long, he left again. She forgave him again. They had their eighth child, another girl. Then he stepped on that dusty road for the last time.

After thirty rainy seasons of not sending so much as a single letter, he sits on a sand-colored recliner with his hands folded on his lap. Luisa stands in the doorway. She'd heard he was coming. She'd also heard his second wife left him.

He clears his throat. "Take me back," he says.

She squints at him for several seconds. He is the only man she ever loved. Yet she remembers how, when one of their sons went missing and she searched for him alone under the moonlight, she whispered her husband's name across the fields too. But he never answered.

"Luisa?" he whispers now.

Her mouth is one straight line. She stares at his ironed shirt and wire-rimmed glasses. He looks old, she thinks.

Finally she tells him, "What you want is a nurse, not a wife."

At that he lowers his bald head.

Later, she would hear that he married a third time and that they had one girl, deaf at birth.

GUATEMALA NOTEBOOKS:
GUATEMALAN HISTORY

- 8,000 years ago. 21 Mayan languages. 60% of country still identifies as Mayan.
- 1521—Spanish arrive. Over 2/3 of Mayan population wiped out first 75 years of Spanish rule.

- 1821—Spain grants independence to all of Central America. September 15. Independence all at once to Central America. Ladinos = mix of indigenous and Spanish heritage. Weren't allowed to own land before because had indigenous blood.

- 1870s. United Fruit Company formed. A privately owned U.S. business owned 75% usable farmland in country. They owned the only railroad in the country, the only port, and most of electricity shares. Nickname: the octopus. In cahoots with military leaders, paid no taxes.

- 1940s. Massive popular uprising, nonviolent. Government overthrown.
- Period of Jacobo Árbenz. Known as "democratic spring."
- Education—first time had a major importance in budget, political plan.
- University granted its autonomy from state. Huge health care reforms too.

- Land Reform—based on Abe Lincoln and Great Depression.
- Any extra scraps of land are up for grabs, but at 25 times price declared on taxes.
- United Fruit Company (UFC) only used 15% of land even though it owned 75%.
- So, UFC tries to convince USA that Guatemala is communist and actually hires Coca-Cola marketing team to paint this picture.

- 1954—CIA organizes and funds a coup d'état in Guatemala.
- Castillo Armas is president. Has a new military dictator.
- Basically took land away from poor campesinos and gave it back to United Fruit Company.

- Nov. 1960—first rebellion/organized movements led by progressive military officials and started a guerrilla movement. Most were initially killed or in exile.

- Finally, 4 organized guerrilla groups formed the URNG. Aiming for a kind of Guatemalan National Revolution.

- Good guys—guerrilleros, fighting for the people.
- Bad guys—corrupt army and government, fighting for select, rich few.

- THE CIVIL WAR. 36 years long. Worst years were from the late 1970s to late 1980s.

- Two distinct tactics: selective repression and fear. Disappeared, tortured, bodies would turn up horribly mutilated, before and after death, to scare you. Fear.

- Brain Drain—at one time only 6 professors running the University in San Carlos.
- Military would kill professors in front of students.
- Even high school teachers, leaders of clubs, etc. assassinated.
- Catholics persecuted too/Liberation theology.

- General Lucas García Ríos Monte. Took it to a new level.
- Implemented "Scorched Earth" Policy—when army goes to rural communities and rounds everyone up after rapes, tortures, and assassinates everyone inside. Kill animals, burn houses, fields so only thing left is "scorched earth."

- 440 towns erased off of the map in a period of 6 years.
- Over 200,000 killed.
- 50,000 disappeared,
- 1.5 million displaced,
- United Nations declared it as genocide,

- R. Montes: "In order to kill the fish, you have to take out the water."

- USA—supported the war the entire time. Provided funding, training (School of the Americas), and weapons.

- They say the trees, the land, have more memories than we do. Witnesses to the truth.

- 1990s. Congress declared we could no longer send "aid" to Guatemala.

- 1996—Peace Accords signed.

- 2006—Ten-year reflection. Things only getting worse. Violence is out of control. More than during the war. 80% population lives in poverty. Only 25% have secure employment.
- 18 murders per day. 44% children are malnourished. People starving to death, this never happened before. A very plentiful country.
- About 50% of population is illiterate. Even though official statement says 30%.

- PLQ—Proyecto Lingüistico Quetzalteco/Language School started in 1988.
- Goals: to teach Spanish but also to share what went down in Guatemala. At first it was a secret school, then moved to a nonprofit in Xela. Where I am writing this now.

A MAP OF THE WORLD

WHEN I WAS IN ninth grade, my father ran away from home. One frostbitten New England morning, he climbed into his gray Toyota and drove toward Guatemala. He left a letter for us written in blue pen on a single sheet of my school notebook paper. Somewhere around D.C. he turned back. I have always wondered how his life, and mine, would be different had he kept driving. His longing has haunted me ever since. It is why I am here in Guatemala, living day to day, page to page. I want to understand how my father could possibly love a country more than his family.

I am sitting in a library in the Western Highlands. Tattered spines of paperbacks line the locked doors of the wooden bookshelves. Paulo Freire. Rigoberta Menchú. John Updike's *Rabbit, Run*. The library is one room with three square wooden tables and, posted on the white wall, a map of the world. It is an upside-down map: North America is in the southern hemisphere; Australia trades places with Europe. A window the size of a door places afternoon light in clean strips across the cool tiles. Outside, clouds cast shadows over the mountains.

The one librarian's name is Aracelis. She is rosy-cheeked and wears a pearl white sweater with a fur collar. Her black hair is thick and long like mine. She hovers over my desk, examines the black marks I have scribbled between the thin tan lines in my leather-bound journal. She leans in. My shoulders tense. I have seen her before. I return to this library like I return to this country, over and over. But today, it's as if my face has a sign that reads, Tell me your story.

"My father lives in the United States, in Arkansas City, and when I was three he left Guatemala to work, but he always called and said he had gifts for us—my mother, my sister, and well . . . my father, for me, he was just everything, hope, a hero, until one day when it was my sister's birthday and we had the cake ready, the food, everything, and the telephone rings and it's him."

All this she tells me in one long black hair of a sentence. She talks with her hands, and her eyes dart left to right. She speaks as if we'd penciled this conversation in our calendar weeks ago, like she'd been practicing it while walking along the narrow, cracked sidewalks in the pink light of sunrise and the orange light of sunset.

"So he says, look, I'm only calling to say that I have another family now. I don't love you anymore, and I'm never returning."

Aracelis and I both nod. Me, side to side, and she, up and down.

"I didn't want to say anything to my sister. So I waited until my mother asked me what was wrong. I had to tell her. My mother sat down and cried. Then my grandparents. My sister. And me."

"Maybe he was lying," I say. "Sometimes life is hard in the U.S. People can't find work. A man can feel like a failure."

"No." Aracelis pulls down her sweater. "After that I didn't want to have anything to do with him. *Yo sufrí.* I even had to go to the hospital—yes."

Through the window I spot an old man pushing a rickety wagon full of empty gas tanks. The shade from his cowboy hat hides his face. The high sun has moved its attention to another latitude, another longitude. Seated at the wooden table, I want to cry, not for Aracelis, not for her father, but for mine. He could not do what other men did, my father, who has been homesick for forty years. And yet a feeling of gratitude swarms me. Thank God he didn't have the guts. Thank God my father came back and that I, his daughter, can relish the warmth of both suns. That is what I felt as I listened to Aracelis that afternoon in the library, when I stared long and hard at the upside-down map.

PART III
AFTER

WORK

THE MORNING I LEFT to house-sit for the famous author on the coast, I searched in the kitchen cupboard at my parents' house for a travel mug lid.

"They want you to *what?*" my father asked.

"House-sit."

It was half past six in the morning on a weekday in July, and he was scrubbing last night's pan in the sink.

"What is that?" he asked.

"It's like babysitting," I said. My father had worked for almost four decades in a computer parts factory after a short stint driving trucks across the country. "Only, I am taking care of the house and not any kids."

Sometimes I felt like my whole life was spent explaining things. I didn't tell him how famous this particular author was or how he had made millions from the only book he'd ever published. Did my father expect that from me? I knew my mother did. Her questions weren't subtle: *How much do you get paid for writing a book? How long does it take? What page are you on now?*

He stared out the window at his garden in the backyard. His tomatoes were doing great.

"Are they paying you?"

"Yeah. Fifty bucks a day. I'll be there for five days."

I could tell what he was thinking. Only in America would people pay to have someone live in their house.

"What do they think? The house is gonna run away?" He placed the clean pan on the stove and reached in the refrigerator for a carton of eggs.

"Maybe," I mumbled and grabbed the directions.

I was grateful for the week of uninterrupted time. I'd been staying on the pullout couch at my parents' house in Massachusetts the last few weeks until the apartment I had sublet was free again. Every night one of them watched TV in the living room and the other in the family room, leaving me to type on my laptop on the dining room table (the only flat surface in the house—my parents didn't own any desks), distracted from the noise coming from two different television sets. Most nights I gave up and microwaved popcorn, or poured cereal and milk into a mug, and plopped down on the couch beside one of them. I ended up watching two or three hours of television when I was supposed to be writing.

I'd cut short my trip to Guatemala, which I'd taken to learn more about my family's history, to improve my Spanish, and to write. Instead, I had scribbled in journals, gotten bit by a dog, and gained eleven pounds. I came home without an idea for a novel, much less a draft. Upon my return to the States, I alternated my days between teaching adults English as a second language at the local college and answering phones at a tile company in Waltham, where my boss referred to most songs that came on the radio as "fuckin' gay." So, yes, this house-sitting gig came at the perfect time. I was hoping that somehow, maybe, miraculously, I could breathe the same air as this famous author and, in five days, at last, begin the work of writing my novel.

I PULLED UP TO the famous author's house. Or at least I thought it was his house. As I kept driving, I realized that the *house* was just the bike shed, mere punctuation to the grand estate. The driveway was at least half a mile long. I could smell the ocean in the distance and hear the gravel crunching underneath the tires. Finally, I parked in front of the blueberry bushes, checked my lip gloss in the rearview mirror. I wore a khaki skirt and a teal polo shirt. Did I look like a respectable house sitter? Preppy enough?

"Hello," the Mr. called from the front door. In my mind he looked like a Mr., like a señor. He had thick black hair, kind eyes, and a firm handshake. He smelled like a spa. A spunky ginger-haired dog barked at his heels. He lifted the dog and allowed her to kiss him on his nose, chin, and mouth. I clenched my toes. At this time in my life I was still afraid of dogs. The Mister led me to the screened-in porch overlooking the bay, where we sat on tan couches and I pretended to love dogs. Bitty sat on my lap. I could feel her little heart beating. She licked my hand, and I resisted the urge to jump.

"In the mornings Bitty likes if you scratch her butt, but by all means, do what you are comfortable with. And if she's looking a little chunky, give her half a turkey meatball. Otherwise, give her the whole one. Help yourself to any alcohol. Don't forget to let me show you how to use the bathtub. The bird you may hear in the morning has black fur on top of its head, kind of like a yarmulke, and it makes a sound like this: mee-UH, mee-UH."

Should I have been taking notes?

"Help yourself to any food, please, and if you want to go for a bike ride, please do. There are maps and trails described in the binder I left on the table."

He stood up suddenly. I followed him around his home—cedar, that was the smell!—and grew mute with envy and shock. The Mister and Mrs. were good people. I could tell from the way he explained things, his concerned and caring instructions, and the way she smiled at me from her gray-blue eyes as she walked down the stairway. He did all the talking while she packed snacks for the car.

"This is the GPS system to use if you want to go to the market. This is how the grill works. This is the outside shower, with biodegradable toiletries. This is the preprogrammed remote control. It's exactly the same as the one upstairs. Are you good with technology? Do you have a Mac? A PC? Are you familiar with iTunes? Yes, of course. This is our music. Have you seen the Animal Planet DVDs? No? Oh! They're really incredible. And I have a job for you. Can you fill this hummingbird container with a quarter cup of sugar and fill it with water up until this line here, and you don't have to go crazy with it, but, oh, you can open the windows like this."

And this and this and this and this and this and this. And this is not your life, but it could be. If you write one best-selling book, you, too, can have a dog and cat that are like a son and daughter, and you can ask people to choose a pair of slippers to use when walking around your house, and you, too, can tell your house sitter that she can help herself to the ripe mango resting in the bamboo woven basket on top of the stainless steel countertop and say, "We've eaten five this week, and they're really delicious. Do you know how to cut a mango?"

Upon seeing that mango, I resisted the urge to burst into tears. I considered its birthplace and its siblings in other places, other countertops, other lands. I thought of the many kinds of mangos that exist and how, before my trip to Guatemala, I had thought there was only one. That mango pulled me back to the many Guatemalan markets, to the *mercado de la democracia* in Quetzaltenango, where women sold everything from cinnamon sticks to shoelaces, from pineapples to live chickens, where over a few months I learned to distinguish the ripe mangos by color and to barter in Spanish and, yes, famous American author, how to cut a mango. I was surprised by my sudden homesickness, which made me return home to my parents, though I'd planned to stay another few months, like a little kid who couldn't make it through the whole sleepover.

After the Mister and Mrs. left, I walked around the house like I was visiting a museum. Oil paintings. Pear-shaped candles in trios. Metallic reading lamps that camouflaged in the natural environment of the living room with the stone walls and massive fireplace. Ceiling-high bookshelves. Oh, the books. Barefoot Contessa cookbooks, hardcovers of *'Tis* and *The Poisonwood Bible*. Copies of *Tender Is the Night* and *1,911 Best Things Anybody Ever Said*. A collection of essays by George Orwell. A dozen books about birds, half a dozen on design and architecture, two on the English language and grammar, one book about cheese, and another titled *What's Wrong with My Dog?* An entire row, bottom shelf, was devoted to the world in the form of atlases.

I opened the refrigerator. It surprised me, it did, that people like this—white people, fit people—had *real* food in their refrigerator and pantries and cupboards and, sigh, bread drawers.

Whole foods. White flour, butter, cream cheese, chocolate chip cookies, Irish oatmeal, oil, vinegar, loaves of fresh rosemary and olive bread, ginger snaps, maple syrup, herbs, a variety of onions arranged in a ceramic bowl so beautifully that I wanted to take a picture. A French press. Ben & Jerry's pints in the freezer beside frosty beer mugs. A bowl of ripe strawberries placed on the middle shelf of the refrigerator. A cheese drawer full of cheeses without labels or expiration dates. Oh, to be a successful author.

I should write. Instead, I wanted to read, make an ice cream sundae, take forty baths, nap in the hammock, sip a martini on the screened-in porch surrounded by lit candles and music I'd never heard before playing through speakers I couldn't see, and maybe even hang out with the dog.

AS A KID I filled pink and purple Lisa Frank notebooks with stories and poems until eighth grade, when I graduated to diaries, and in high school, leather-bound journals I purchased with birthday and holiday money. In college I didn't major in English. I wrote, but I didn't have the guts to call myself a writer yet. I took a writing class or two. Narrative Non-fiction. The Short Story. The same tenured professor taught both. I wrote about my cousins in East L.A. who said *hella* and *fool*, and I wrote a short story about a teenage girl who shoplifted and got caught on Valentine's Day. What did I know? I knew that I had never met a writer, that authors didn't look like me, and that writers were poor. Except *this* guy. His writing studio was bigger than my apartment.

THE SEPTEMBER AFTER I graduated from college, I enrolled in a local creative writing class held on Saturday mornings at a church in Stoneham, Massachusetts. It seemed like something writers did, take classes. We were told to bring a piece of writing to the first session. When I arrived, I saw elderly people gathered around the square wooden table. It was, I quickly realized, a senior citizen writing class. And it was too late to back out. The man to my right read a short essay about a time he had proctored an SAT exam in a gymnasium and a boy kept sneaking bites of a ham sandwich from under his desk. I wasn't sure where the story led. Maybe I had missed part of it because I was debating whether to read my own essay about getting drunk and kissing two boys in one night at a party in Boston. Jacqueline, the lively ninety-something-year-old instructor, looked at me with her watery eyes and suggested I go next. One man pushed his chair closer to the table. The room smelled like Pledge.

"Oh, I don't need to read," I said.

"Don't be silly," she said. "It's why we're here."

I cleared my throat. How did I get myself into these situations? Were there no other writing classes in the state of Massachusetts? My roommates were sleeping in on this weekend morning, and here I was sharing a tale of promiscuity with strangers, senior citizen strangers.

After I finished reading, everyone was silent. Jacqueline asked if she could see it. So I tore out the page from my journal and handed it to her. She grinned like a schoolgirl. She never gave it back.

THAT FIRST DAY IN the famous author's house I couldn't focus. My laptop was baking somewhere on the backseat in my hot car parked on the circular driveway. I spent those first sunny hours fiddling with the house music system—soon discovering that I loved Amos Lee—and exploring all the rooms, including the personal gym in the basement and the upstairs bathroom with a special Japanese bathtub. I read about it in the binder the Mister had left on the dining room table. There was a whole chapter on what to do if the power went out. I would have to turn red knobs counterclockwise and such so the hot water wouldn't explode or something. I prayed it wouldn't rain while I was there, and not because I wanted to use one of the spare bikes (who had spare bikes?) in the bike shed and get in touch with the marshy environment or whatever, but so that I wouldn't have to reference this particular chapter.

AFTER THAT WRITING CLASS in Stoneham I didn't look into other creative writing courses for a while. I joined Teach For America. I needed a job. I needed money. And I figured teaching would help fill the well that I'd draw from later in my future writing work. So I moved to California and became a third-grade teacher. Twenty-two little bodies greeted me as Miss De Leon each morning at a San Jose elementary school. One of my students had a reading disability. He spelled *they* as *da* and *teacher* as *chicher*. After school, young and exhausted parents often told me their stories. They had cousins in Mexico and Vietnam praying dawn until dusk for visas to the United States, an uncle who had worked as a physics professor at home and now sold Mary Kay products door-to-door with his wife. Entire families rented single rooms in three-bedroom houses because it was all they could afford. On September 11, 2002, the kids drew towers with tangerine orange flames and black clouds. We made a classroom Bill of Rights. (Isaac's suggestion: The Right to Recess.) Teaching devoured my time. I stopped writing. I stopped reading, save for *Pedagogy of the Oppressed* and a young adult novel titled *Esperanza Rising*.

During these years as an elementary school teacher and full-time graduate student, I kept deodorant inside my glove compartment. I used teacher discounts everywhere, from the laundromat to the bar. I chose sleep over sex. A case of Diet Coke, batches of ungraded spelling quizzes, Expo markers, flip-flops, and all kinds of jackets—fleece, rain, wool, denim—piled in the backseat of my green Ford Escape. I was supposed to have already published a book by now, wasn't I? My journal gathered dust somewhere underneath my unmade bed.

One gray San Francisco afternoon later that semester, the director of the Master of Arts in Teaching program handed me a tissue in his office. His name was Herb Kohl, and his white hair stuck out like Einstein's. "What are you *not* doing that you *need* to be doing?" he asked.

"Writing," I said. I was a mess of red seated in the folding chair—red puffy eyes, red jacket, chipped red nail polish. Writing was the way I always brought myself back to an equilibrium. I loved doing it. It made me feel better. Was it Gloria Steinem who said that when writing, she didn't feel like she should be doing anything else? Me too.

"Well do it then," Herb said.

He organized a small group of writers to meet at his apartment, located at the top of a hill in the Mission. Eric, a teacher at an alternative high school, usually wrote about his students. Jerica wrote about growing up in Stockton with her racist grandmother. I wrote about my mother and Guatemala. We met on Sunday afternoons when the sunlight pressed against the tall window shades and dust danced in the air. Other people joined our writing group now and then, but mostly it was Eric, Jerica, Armando, Herb, and me. Armando was the person guaranteed to make everyone cry every time. He pretended he didn't have anything to read, and then he'd drag out his laptop covered with peeling stickers. We'd cross and uncross our legs while he searched for the right document. Armando was a six-foot, two-hundred-something-pound Mexican man with tattoos and a buzz cut. He wore glasses, jeans, and a tucked-in T-shirt, and he'd ask us for advice on how to get his ninth graders to dig *Romeo and Juliet*. Armando always wrote about his family. He wrote about his mother and how she smuggled *nopales* across the U.S. border by wrapping pieces of the prickly pear inside her bra. He wrote about his father chasing the hearse by foot that carried his teenage daughter, Armando's sister, all the way to the cemetery. He wrote about visiting his brother in the prison cafeteria on Thanksgiving. And he wrote about his first love. Whenever his voice cracked while he was reading, he'd pause before saying, "Aw shit."

One time Herb showed us a copy of his latest manuscript, with dozens of comments scribbled in the margins from his editor in New York City. "Look really hard," he said. "If you want to be a writer, look at what it takes. It's hard work. It's not all fancy book tours." He passed around the stack of pages. I held it in my arms like an infant. I'd never seen a book like that before, before it was a book.

After California, after I moved back to Massachusetts to teach for the Boston Public Schools, I turned twenty-six. I rented a studio apartment in Back Bay because a part of me felt like I should, like it was something Carrie Bradshaw from *Sex in the City* would do, and she was a writer, so . . . The Boston Center for Adult Education was around the corner from my apartment. It offered classes in everything from an introduction to fencing to watercolors, to fundamentals of investing, and to, yes, creative writing. One afternoon I decided to sign up for Memoir Writing, smiling after I hung up the phone with the lady who took my credit card number.

We met on Tuesday nights. The classes were held in the historic Gamble Mansion on Commonwealth Avenue. It was built in 1904 and was the home of Mr. and Mrs. Walter Baylies and their six children until 1936. On the first night, I made my way up the creaking spiral staircase to the classroom, which was really a small annex on the top floor. The angled ceiling and rectangular wooden table with centuries worth of nicks on its maple surface made me feel as if I was doing something important. Four other women, all white, sat around the table. None of us looked up.

The instructor introduced herself and then asked us to go around the room and do the same. Our first prompt: write about a trip you have taken that had significant emotional impact. I returned the following week with six stapled photocopies of my paper. I stared out at the gray city heat through the smudged window, the sound of the air conditioner rattling in the background, while four strangers discussed my work. They said, "Your mom is funny," and "I went to Costa Rica once." They pronounced Guatemala, G-uuuaa-*te*-maaaala. Their written comments were helpful, their edits thoughtful and precise. With multicolored pens I wrote down the titles and authors of every book they mentioned.

"Oh, that reminds me of Lorrie Moore."

"I looooove Grace Paley."

"Have you ever read *Eat, Pray, Love?*"

"Yes! I loved it."

"You would like Jeannette Walls."

The other students mentioned authors like they were old friends from camp. I didn't dare admit I hadn't heard of a single one.

"I like the book *Drown* by Junot Díaz," I said.

"I've heard of him," one woman said.

"And Frank McCourt."

"Oh, yeah, he's good," they said.

I attended every one of the six classes on Tuesday nights in July and August that summer as if my life depended on it, as if all the lives of the people in my stories did. When the class was over, we exchanged email addresses and promised to keep in touch, which we never did.

A FEW MONTHS AFTER the Boston Center for Adult Education class, on my way to catch the train one afternoon, I rushed past an Emerson College building on Tremont Street. My only other association with Emerson was that my aunt used to clean the dorm bathrooms. The next week I returned to that building, stepped inside, and walked out with a receipt for enrollment in a fiction class.

At Emerson we met in a spacious, carpeted room with clean, rectangular tables arranged in a giant square U. The lighting reminded me of swanky bars that served overpriced martinis, which made everyone look *writerly*. The instructor, Ben, was tall and white haired, and he wore jeans and a flannel button-down shirt to every class; he had sympathetic eyes and spoke about a tenth of the amount Laurie had spoken in the memoir class. Maybe he was burnt out from teaching and only taught this class for the extra money. He *did* have a hole in his jeans at the knee. Most of us arrived straight from work. People ranged in age from twenty-something to one retired Jewish woman with frosted highlights in her wild brown hair.

Like in the other class, everyone was white. We chewed Subway sandwiches and crunched on Doritos while discussing pieces from the *O. Henry Prize Stories*. I devoured work from authors who, again, at the time, I had never heard of: Ron Rash, Sherman Alexie, Elizabeth Stuckey-French. Sometimes people brought in chocolate chip cookies or Hershey's Kisses. We sipped coffee. Always coffee. The whiff of French vanilla permanently in the air.

I considered dropping the course three different times. If I did so by a specific deadline, I could get most of my money back. One cold October evening I decided that this was it, this would be my last class. The price tag was just too crazy expensive. For this class I paid what my father earned in a month (after taxes). I walked toward the Emerson building, too hungry to wait until the break to purchase a slimy turkey and cheese sub and a large coffee. So I went to the nearest restaurant, a Vietnamese fast-food place. One thousand bucks. That equaled a hell of a lot of takeout. I could fly a couple of relatives from Guatemala to Boston for that amount. I could buy a new computer.

Smells of lemongrass and ginger greeted me as I pulled open the glass door to the Vietnamese place. I spotted my teacher picking at a stack of fried noodles with a white plastic fork on a paper plate. He squinted in my direction.

"Hey," he said.

"Oh, hi." I pulled my jacket closer, nodding like an idiot, and wished he would say something else. He didn't. I smiled and nodded a final time before making my way to the counter, where I ordered a number seven with extra hot sauce on the side.

"To go?" the man asked.

"To go," I said, my stomach growling in disagreement.

I stared at the photos mounted on the wall above me, pictures of plated dishes garnished with mint leaves and curly strips of mango.

"How do you like the class so far?" Ben asked from his booth ten feet away.

"A lot," I said. Even in my midtwenties, I still turned nervous when talking to teachers outside the classroom. And it was like I could sense that he could sense that maybe I was going to quit tonight. I mean, I was.

He wiped his mouth with a paper napkin. "I'm glad you're in the class."

"Thanks."

"Number seven!"

THAT NIGHT BEN GAVE us an in-class writing assignment. We wrote for twenty minutes. The tall guy with blue eyes in the red-and-white-striped polo shirt raised his hand to share first. I thought he would suck, but he didn't. He was really good, and I told myself there was absolutely no way that I was going to share. I couldn't wait to eat my dinner. I had resisted the urge to untie that tight plastic knot the entire first hour of class. I wouldn't be *that ethnic girl* eating her *ethnic food* and getting greasy fingerprints all over the copies of the stories and the corners of the thin gray pages of the O. *Henry* book.

"Jennifer?" Ben asked. He never wasted a single word. Maybe that was why he was such a good writer.

I didn't want to share. But I gripped my notebook and read from the first sentence: "I was surprised to see my father."

At the end of class—my last, remember—a lady stopped me at the elevator and said she liked what I had shared tonight.

"You did? Really? Because I was thinking of dropping the course. Do you think I should?"

She wore an emerald green cardigan set and brown slacks. That night, she had read a piece about a woman whose husband had given her an eighteen-dollar bottle of Absolut for their tenth anniversary present.

"Oh, you definitely should be in this class," she said. "What you read tonight was really good. You seem like you have a lot to offer. It's worth it."

Had I imagined that she said that last part? *It's worth it.*

"Thanks," I said.

I thought of my parents, how they left their homeland of Guatemala in the seventies and moved to Boston for a better life.

Growing up, every restaurant meal, good pair of shoes, Trapper Keeper, or vacation was a contrast to their own childhoods and an opportunity for them to share their struggles with my sisters and me. "Find a job where you don't have to work with your hands," my father would tell us.

I never considered that my stories had actual worth or that I could make an honest living from writing. A master of fine arts program? At first I talked myself out of it: I could read fiction on my own. I could ride the T to the Boston Public Library and sit in the high-ceilinged room with endless rows of wooden tables and green desk lamps and read all the books I had never taken seriously in high school and college. Twain. Swift. Flaubert. Joyce. Woolf. Nabokov. I would reread *Catch-22* and *Slaughterhouse Five* and *The Bell Jar*. Look up that author, Jeannette Walls. Get on the waiting list for *Eat, Pray, Love* (it must be good if forty-seven people were on the waiting list). After a couple of years I enrolled in a fiction graduate program in Boston. Then I quit after the first semester.

THE WEATHER TURNED. I sat, writing in my journal, on the famous author's L-shaped couch inside the beautiful mansion, the one that his children and grandchildren will inherit for no reason other than having been born into his family. The sky bruised. The barking dog ran in circles around my feet. Day three and I hadn't left the house. Why would I? There was food, a home gym, Wi-Fi, and an ocean view. The house phone rang and startled me awake from a nap. It was the Mister. He said something about a storm coming and could I be sure to close the windows. No problem. That evening the wind howled and the sky flashed with lightning that sent the dog whimpering underneath the couch. I drank red wine. Wrote a poem for my best friend's upcoming wedding. My mother called.

"How can you be there all by yourself? What are you doing? Can you come home for one night?" She passed the phone to my father.

"Lock all the doors," he said in a tone like I was in big trouble.

"It's just rain," I said, and hung up.

My mother's question stung. What are you doing? I was working. There were people in the world that worked as lawyers, executives, and doctors. There were people who worked at banks, at stores, prisons. What was my work? Writing? Technically, my work was house-sitting and feeding pets and watering plants, but I was also gearing up to write something big and important and *literary*—and I relied on this space and solitude in which to do it. Maybe my mother didn't understand that, or maybe I was just full of shit. I had space and solitude in Guatemala, and yet I came home without a novel. And now here I was, in a gorgeous home, all the space and solitude I wanted, and still I found it difficult to write.

Deep down I knew I had a novel in me. I didn't know what it was about yet, but I knew it existed. In Guatemala I had put so much pressure on myself to write it because I had never had this much free time. I felt a tremendous amount of expectation weighing on me. My parents never had six days to themselves, let alone six months. On vacations my father would build a shed in the backyard, repaint the porch, or tinker with the car engines. My mother hated to miss a single day of work. Not once do I remember her taking a sick day. Yet there I was, in their native country, with all their support and faith, and I felt close to drowning with doubt. Some nights, before I fell asleep, I prayed for my health, then for my novel. I didn't want to look back on this time and be swarmed by the agonizing feeling that I'd somehow wasted it. I couldn't get rid of that voice in my head that constantly reminded me of what a privilege it was to be here, to be a girl wanting to write. I could not return home empty-handed.

The storm outside thickened, and the power went out. I found a flashlight and fumbled through the section of the house manual that I'd dreaded. The last thing I needed was for the Mister to come home and discover there was water spilling from the upstairs bathroom. I read the directions out loud (somehow I thought that helped) and managed to turn off what I needed to turn off. I was suddenly tired in a way I hadn't been in days.

I WOULDN'T REALIZE IT until much later, after I had really looked at my journals from Guatemala, reread them and saw there were several promising pieces in there—seeds of stories, mini-essays, and even future books; after I took those pages and rewrote them and submitted them to literary magazines; after I won first place in a contest, won one thousand dollars, the same amount I had paid for the Emerson class so long ago. After I reenrolled in my MFA program, even if it meant graduating later than planned; after my parents and *abuela* and cousins and their three kids came to my thesis reading; after I became a professor of creative writing; and after I won residencies and fellowships and prizes and published a book and gave speeches around the country my parents moved to so long ago, this country where every day feels like the first day and the last day. All that time I had been writing in my journal and writing in my head and writing on whatever scraps of paper I could find in my purse or my car, but I didn't yet understand how these separate islands could morph into a bigger island, into a small world. The work of writing does not look like it looks on TV. That summer, while house-sitting for a famous author, all I knew was that I wanted to keep going, that if I squinted just enough, at the end of this dock I could see another dock, and another, and another.

It was time to go.

In the morning I cleaned the house, washed the towels, worked out once more in the basement gym. I left a note for the Mister and his wife. I gathered the last of my things—journals, rough drafts, workshop stories, and lists. Words surrounded me. Post-it notes that read meeting/conflict/resolution; Mom—detail about pears as aphrodisiacs—use!; soy milk, nuts, salsa. Who knew how I would ever stitch together these separate patches, how my memories and ideas would ever form a cohesive book, but in the meantime, I would just continue to write it all down. Chop the wood. Gather the clay. What is that quote by Zora Neale Hurston? "There are years that ask questions and years that answer."

By January I was writing one thousand words a day. It was a practice I'd read about in a book about living a literary life. I decided to try it. Each day the words came easier. Some days I wrote two thousand words. Other days, eight hundred. By February I had forty thousand words of a first draft of my novel. It was impossible then to know where my words would eventually land, but I can say with more certainty now that I no longer doubt this work or its worth. Who are they to say what we hold in our hands?

HAPPY NEW YEAR

I T SNOWED ALL DAY, so my mother was wondering if the New Year's Eve party was still on. It wasn't a party for us to attend; it was a party for us to *work*. The hosts: an elderly couple one town over from my parents' house. We got the job from a friend of a lady whose house my mother had cleaned for twenty-two years. I agreed to keep my mom company on this night because, after all, it was New Year's Eve and I would have hated for her to be alone. That was what I told myself. The truth was that I had been back from my trip to Guatemala for several months now and was still feeling stalled out, like I didn't know what I was doing in life. To some extent I knew this was normal for a twenty-something-year-old, but I couldn't help feeling lame anyway. Although, truthfully, I'd *had* my fair share of New Year's Eve festivities. Twenty-eight of them. I'd watched the ball drop in Times Square while sharing a bottle of cheap champagne with friends. I'd savored the simple New Year's Eve with a boyfriend and a pile of rented DVDs. I'd slept through New Year's Eve celebrations blaring on the television screen when I lived in California and was still on East Coast time. But I had never worked with my mother on New Year's Eve. This would be a first.

My father gave us a ride. It was dark when we pulled into the retirement community made up of perfectly arranged condominiums that resembled the miniature houses of Monopoly.

The snow was thick. He told us to call him when we were ready to be picked up.

"You sound like a shuttle van driver," I said.

"Shut the door," he said.

Feliz Año Nuevo, I mouthed as he peeled his way past snow-frosted bushes that looked like vanilla cupcakes.

Was it too late to go back? A part of me wanted to dive in the car and ditch my mom. The older I got, the more introverted I'd become. Maybe *introverted* was just a euphemism for *depressed*. Because I had come home from Guatemala earlier than planned, my apartment was still being sublet so I had to stay with my parents for two months, on their living room sofa bed to be exact. I had also come home to friends' wedding engagements, bridal showers, and baby showers. Life suddenly felt like the props on the set had changed and everyone else was dressed in new costumes and they all knew their lines and I was standing in the shadows, wanting to run in a new direction, any direction, and yet feeling as if my feet were bolted to the floor. That was when I started seeing my new therapist, Caitlyn.

Caitlyn was only a few years older than me and had silky brown hair down to her shoulders. During our first meeting, while I sat on the gray suede couch in her dimly lit office, the sound of water trickling over stones in the distance, she explained that we each lived our lives according to this book, or a story, a narrative. Immediately I perked up.

"We have ideas and major story lines we feel we will carry out, live. There are, however, some past chapters that we need to close.

And we can learn a lot from looking at the maybe unexpected story lines—or what we wouldn't look to first." I didn't totally know what she was saying, but it sounded good and warm and true. She also said we needed to be more forgiving and kind to ourselves. She said that I sounded like a motivated, bright woman and that I was going to be okay. I told her about my anxiety surrounding making decisions. "Menus?" she asked. "Yup, that's fine." But then I told her about Staples and how I stood in the folders section of the aisle for a good twenty minutes deciding which ones to get: manila, pastel, primary colors. I told her that in Spanish, the word *hubiera* lingered over my spirit like a dark cloud. *Should have.*

"Hmm," she said. She wrote on a yellow pad while I sank into the couch, hugging my Nalgene bottle to my core.

"Why do you think it was so difficult to choose which folders to buy?"

Had she ever *been* to Staples? "Well," I said, "I think it's connected to my fear of making wrong choices, my immense fear of regret. Maybe that's why the folders are such a big deal. I am afraid of making the wrong choice, life choice, path—there are so many avenues I am confronted with suddenly. I always thought I'd be living in Africa or something. I mean, not forever. Okay, I'd like to be married, have kids, a house—but *later.* And now all of a sudden that's like HERE." I put my open palm right up to my nose.

She winced. Scribbled furiously.

"How's your sleep?"

"Fine."

"It's so hard," she said.

THE ELDERLY COUPLE GREETED us at the door. Because my mother and I were fifteen minutes late (we were always late), they didn't waste any time. "This is where the Saran wrap is; this is where the recycling goes; this is where we store the extra bottles of gin and ginger ale and caffeine-free Diet Coke." The Mr. and Mrs. had thought of everything: wicker trays for guests to carry their meals into the living room, folded napkins lining the stacked paper plates, a variety of easily chewed and digested options from potato salad to sweet kaiser rolls to applesauce with cinnamon sugar sprinkled on top. "Here, here, here," they said. My mother, the most confident woman in the world, nodded as she played with her knuckles. I felt like a bird in the corner, watching, blinking.

"All the guests are our neighbors," the Mrs. said. She explained that they all lived in the same retirement community and did activities together—bingo, book club, gin and tonic night.

"Oh," I said, louder than intended. *Old people* was probably written all over my face. I had only meant to nod. She looked at me. I looked at her.

"What about drinks?" my mother asked.

The bar was the kitchen island and the centerpiece of the party. During the first hour alone I refilled the silver ice bucket three times.

"Is there any more Riesling?"

"They got any rum?"

"Do you know if they have cold beers in the fridge?"

"Is this my drink—do you know where I left my drink?"

"Can you open this?"

A short guy with three white hairs on his head asked the last question. He was the one who, when my mother and I were collecting coats as the guests made their entrances—changing shoes, asking for a tissue, lifting their tiered trays of crudités and lemon squares for all to admire—still had the price tag stuck on his shirt. I didn't have the heart to tell him. But my mother did. He wasn't the slightest bit embarrassed. He just chuckled and walked away in his squeaky shoes. I wished I could be more like that.

After I had returned from my trip to Guatemala, I was in a sort of PTSD state for a while; I mean, there was so much to process from those few months living in Central America, in my parents' homeland, in a country I had grown up hearing so much about but never fully experienced by myself. Looking back, I think I was in some kind of emotional moratorium. Don't you love how I come up with so many euphemisms for *depressed?* What was there to be depressed about? I had gone, with my own money and on my own will, to live in another part of the world to learn more about Guatemala, to write, to improve my Spanish. This was living, wasn't it? I was a writer. Writers needed to travel and write. And I did that. I filled journals and notebooks and started endless documents on my laptop. I mean, I didn't have a concrete product as in a manuscript or a book or, say, an idea for a book. But I was there. I was writing. Sort of. No, I was. See the indecisiveness? This is what it was for me when I returned home to Boston: I felt like my friends and coworkers and just *everybody else* was moving on, living their lives, checking off boxes of life accomplishments, and here I was, marching in place at best. See the glass half-empty? That was my mood that year.

Even after I moved back to Boston, I still felt out of it, like I couldn't get back into a groove. I was newly twenty-nine, single, in a graduate program for creative writing, and still babysitting and tutoring to make money. What the hell was I doing with my life? What were my plans? Wasn't I, as my aunt in Guatemala had asked with the concern of a thousand nuns, planning on getting married and having kids? I mean, sure, eventually. I mean, maybe. If the right person came along. I wasn't going to marry someone just for the sake of being married. The closest I'd come to it was with my former boyfriend, whom I dated for—depending on your math—four, five, or six years. At one point we imagined our lives together, our kids, our careers, all of it. But things happen— moving across the country for graduate programs, new jobs, parent illnesses, arguments that leave scars, doubts that grow no matter how many times you try to smother them.

After I returned from Guatemala and moved back into my apartment in Boston, I had no real schedule, never mind a *writing* schedule. I was floating and falling, being carried like a brown leaf in the wind. Some weekdays I would run the most bizarre errands smack in the middle of the day. Once, I drove to the Gap in Coolidge Corner on a Wednesday at noon and tried on ten different pairs of jeans. Another time I frantically called bookstores and asked about this one novel, *The Yacoubian Building*, because a woman in a writing workshop had recommended it to me two years ago but I was just going through the notes and had come across her suggestion. Yes, Brookline Booksmith had it, yes, please put it on hold, thank you, I'll be right over. The next day I continued digging through the notes. Oh, ZZ Packer mentioned

Story Structure Architect. So I called Barnes and Noble. Same exact conversation as above, and thirty-five minutes later, I was riding up the store's main entrance escalator like my life depended on it. Because that is what it felt like at the time, like my life depended on it. I couldn't see further into the future: only that one task in that one hour. If I did that, I felt, I could do more. Maybe anything. It was a deep sense of control I was seeking. I know that now. But at the time, I was nothing but frantic.

At the Gap that day, none of the jeans had fit (of course), but I bought a pair anyway (of course) for way too much money (fifty-eight dollars) and then drove to Boomerangs, a thrift store, on Centre Street in Jamaica Plain. By then it was almost half past one in the afternoon. Looking back, I cringe at the hours I "wasted" when I could have been writing at my IKEA desk in my apartment. But that day I tried on ten more pairs of jeans (I could have purchased all of them for less than the price of one pair from the Gap, which days later still sat in a blue plastic bag on the passenger seat of my car). At the thrift store none of the jeans fit either. I left, lathered with more despair that I thought possible for a short-sleeve-shirt kind of day in October. I mean, I never wanted to kill myself, but at moments like that I desperately wished there were another alternative between being dead and alive.

AT THE NEW YEAR's party, the bottles of liquor arranged on the marble countertop took me on a tour of my twenties. The squarish green gin bottle made me think of that night in San Francisco when I puked in the bar bathroom because I had drunk too many Cosmopolitans. The Bacardí Limón bottle reminded me of parties in college and recapping the night with friends over a two-hour brunch the next day. The SKYY vodka invited the image of my girlfriends underneath the blur of lights at the Roxy the night we thought it was a good idea to flash the bartender for free shots. The chilled Chardonnay bottle, snug in its ceramic wine holder, took me back to the mismatching plates at dinner parties with roommates in our first apartment out of college. Then, I spotted it. Bottle of red: Mondavi. I was yanked back to the wine vineyard in Napa Valley that my ex-boyfriend and I visited during the first month of our relationship when everything was sun-kissed with newness. That was a long time ago. What wasn't a long time ago? Last month, when he and I had met up in New York City and a giant question mark lodged between us: Will this work, again?

"I HATE TO BOTHER you," the Mrs. interrupted me. It was a funny thing to say because I wasn't actually doing anything. I was standing in the kitchen, leaning against the counter, staring at the wall. Could she tell I was thinking about my ex-boyfriend? My ears felt hot.

"Can you help me move the folding chairs to the main living room? We are about to start the Yankee Swap."

On my way to the living room my mom pointed her thumb at me and said, "She wants her forty!" And I knew she meant forty bucks as in two crisp twenty-dollar bills the couple would hand to us each at the end of the night, but the guests just looked at us strangely. I told my mom that "a forty" meant a forty-ounce malt liquor beer. She didn't care. I unfolded the chairs and lined them up in rows. Couples sat together. One had a walker. Another sat on the rug, and I admit I found this a little surprising. Yoga? One woman sat alone, and although she was surrounded by people, she had that aura of solitude—her prolonged stares, the way she held her clear plastic cup and rubbed her napkin like a rabbit's foot, the counterclockwise motion of her ankle as she sat cross-legged on the ottoman. She caught my eye and I looked away.

During the Yankee Swap my mother and I got a break. We ate roast beef on rye bread. We sat at the round wooden table in the kitchen and spoke in Spanish. I could tell she was a little buzzed. Earlier, the Mr. had told us we could help ourselves to anything we wanted. My mom had been drinking Pinot Grigio all night like it was soda, her glass filled with clinking ice cubes. If I tried, I could probably count the beads of sweat forming on her cheeks and nose. I sensed the conversation turning toward my ex-boyfriend. She knew that he and I had been talking lately. My mother had never really liked him. He was a mama's boy, said the woman who only had daughters. But now, as I faced thirty, maybe she was thinking she liked him enough. Funny how she was the brazen one in the extended family, the one who shoved her daughters into the world, out of church, onto college campuses, all the while urging us *not* to settle down too early, all to allow us a freedom she never had, always wanted. And now *she* was the one eyeing store window displays of baby mannequins wearing pastel dresses and in her "oh so wounded" way asking, "Won't my daughters make me a grandmother someday?"

My mother wiped the crumbs from the table with her palm.
"So where is he? I mean, how is he?"

"He's traveling for work," I said. It was true.

"Where?"

"Africa," I lied.

"Oh, wow."

IN A SLOW MOMENT, I leaned against the marble kitchen counter—
again—and popped lemon squares into my mouth like they were
Skittles. Then I moved on to white chocolate–covered almonds.
I could hear guests in the living room laughing. Was I jealous
of them? Maybe a bit. Next I reached for a handful of peanut
M&M's. While working hard on building my sugar coma, I noticed
a handsome old man unhinge himself from a salt-and-pepper-
haired trio. He approached me. Should I pretend I don't speak
English? I didn't feel like chatting. Besides, I was chewing. He
was dressed in a fitted red cashmere sweater. I wondered if his
wife had picked it out for him.

"Well, you look interesting," he said.

I smiled in that *Oh boy, here we go* kind of a way.

"I mean, you look a hell of a lot more interesting than anyone
in here."

Was he drunk?

His wife fixed her eyes on us from across the kitchen. She
looked like she was half-listening to a woman wearing a fur coat.
I knew this particular woman was his wife because when they
came in together and I took their coats, only he said thank you.

She wore too much makeup and had a modern short haircut, dyed auburn.

"I'm Dora's daughter," I said. "I'm a teacher. I live in Boston."

"Where'd you go to school?"

"Connecticut College."

"Oh yeah? You liked it?"

"Loved it."

He took a sip of his clear bubbly drink. "You did good, kid."

Had I? Done good? I was twenty weekends away from turning thirty, yet I felt like I was nine, hanging out with my mom on New Year's Eve. For forty bucks.

"Thank you," I said.

"And where is your boyfriend tonight?"

"In Africa."

"What?"

"I don't have a boyfriend."

"What?"

"I DON'T HAVE A BOYFRIEND."

He leaned back. "Good for you," he said. "You don't need that bullshit."

"Thank you," I said again.

The woman wearing the ginger-colored mink interrupted us, announcing: "I bought this coat in 1987." She eyed me up and down. "You have any cigarettes?"

"No, sorry."

She looked disappointed. "I'm loaded. You?"

Someone yelled from the hall. "Twenty minutes 'til midnight!"

I took that as my excuse to leave the kitchen. In the hallway I saw five ladies clustered on the carpeted steps. They were in that cloud of girl talk, and I was now officially jealous of them.

"Where are you going?" my mother asked. I ignored her, making my way to the bathroom down the hall, past the popular puff on the stairs.

This was exactly why I didn't like visiting my parents on the weekends. I always felt like I was under a microscope, and I could not lie to my mother. It was like she would *know*. It was like she *already knew*. It hurt me to think that she worried about me and if I'd find someone. I couldn't stand to listen to her stories a minute more, about the little boy adopted from Guatemala who lived across the street, or about the woman at the bank whose daughter just got engaged. I avoided going to my parents' house, avoided talking to them. To my mother especially, I was so rude on the phone. You already told me that! To which she replied, simply, "Oh." What was my problem? I missed being in love. In Wednesday love, not just Saturday love. Thing was, I was so scared to date. I found something wrong with everyone because I found something wrong with myself. Lately I felt altogether confused and lost, and I hated that I didn't know what else to do in my life. It was taking its toll. I looked and felt old. When was it my turn to find the love of my life? What was God's plan for me? Did I disappoint God at some point or something? Was I mean? Selfish? If I was, I wish I could take it all back. Tomorrow was a new year. I would wake up and make a healthy breakfast. Yes! Greek yogurt, Weetabix, frozen strawberries, and almonds. Brew coffee. I would do laundry, clean my room, clean the living room, figure out some stuff. I'd even like to clean the inside of my car. Make a novel wall. You know, like really think through story lines. Keep the tension moving throughout, like in *The Yacoubian Building*. Truth was, the sadness was creeping behind my eyes, and no makeup could get rid of it. I didn't know this age, this part of life, was going to be this difficult. I didn't yet have a rhythm—well, there was the rhythm of trying over and over again. That counted as a rhythm, I hoped.

AT THE PARTY I refilled the ice bucket, wiped coasters, collected crumpled napkins, stirred the honey mustard so it didn't look congealed. I told my mom we were low on seltzer, and I stepped into the garage, whispering a little prayer. *Make this year different.* I considered calling my ex-boyfriend, the one who had recently resurfaced. In an email to me a few weeks before he wanted to know: "Has the boat left the dock?" I typed, deleted, retyped: "I don't know."

"Meet me at the Hudson Hotel in New York City," he wrote.

"Okay."

I told my therapist, Caitlyn, about the plan to meet him in Manhattan for the weekend. She crossed and uncrossed her legs. "How do you feel about it?"

I shrugged. We sat in silence. "I guess . . . ," I said. She leaned forward, and I realized that she genuinely wanted to know, as if I really were a story in a book and this moment was a major plot point: What was going to happen next? "I guess . . . I feel like . . . it's kind of like . . . I'm waiting on this dock. And a familiar boat is approaching. I know this boat. It's not perfect, but it's a good boat. Mostly. And if it passes me by and I don't get on this boat, then that's it, I mean, I'm left alone on the dock. And the boat might not come back, like probably ever. And I'll be stranded on this dock forever, alone."

"What about the possibility of other boats coming along?"

"Yeah." What else was I supposed to say?

"Or . . ." Caitlyn shifted her weight in her therapist chair. "You could get off the dock and take your own boat into the water and see what's out there. In the water, I mean."

I knew what she meant. On a literal level, she meant: leave your couch on the weekends. On a philosophical level, she meant: there is a time for experiencing a dark night of the soul, but then turn the light on, okay? Even though in that exact moment I wasn't able to absorb the optimism in her point, it was a good one nonetheless. I put it in my pocket for later, like a mint on the way out of a restaurant.

I didn't tell my mother or my sisters or any friends that I was taking a bus to New York one Friday to meet my former boyfriend. I begged that bone-chilling December night for answers. On my way up the fancy hotel lobby's backlit escalator, my fake Fendi bag tugging my right shoulder, I mentally stitched together all the treadmill miles I'd logged thinking about him, my sore muscles, how my ribs had become visible through fitted tops at one point. Then I remembered the worst fight we'd ever had. *Do you really think that when you die, anyone is going to care about what books you've written?* The escalator spit me onto the polished hardwood of the second floor. That weekend in Manhattan, I let him buy me martinis and lattes and Indian curry wraps before he put me in a cab headed for the bus station on Monday morning. I waved at him through the window and felt a glacier thawing on my chest.

FIVE MINUTES UNTIL MIDNIGHT. The hallway bathroom was occupied, so I walked toward the back bedroom to use the master bathroom. The mountain of black coats on the bed stared at me as I stepped inside and shut the door behind me. All these people at the party have lived almost triple the amount of years I have. Did they have regrets? Did they ever wonder, what if I had pursued that one relationship? What if I had run away? Quit my job? Left the country? Did I settle? Appreciate what I had? And me: Why did I have to wonder if someone and something better were always just around the corner? Was that it? Or was it just a matter of timing? That was all life was, wasn't it? A trick of timing, over and over again. I could hear the old people partying in the living room, cheering and counting down: three, two, one! The black-and-white clock on the bedside table struck twelve. I thought about what Caitlyn had said. Make your own boat. I knew in that moment that *this* is what I would regret most: not making my own boat, or at least not trying to anyway. I wanted to be like that old guy earlier in the evening who ripped the price tag off his sweater and kept on moving. Because, as cliché as it is, life was short. Right?

When I came back to the living room, it was only a few minutes past midnight. As if they had curfews, the guests were frantically searching for platters they came in with and they were busy securing Yankee Swap gifts into shiny silver and gold gift bags.

"Where were you?" my mother asked.

"In the bathroom."

She slivered her eyes, handed me her cell phone; it was warm in my palm. "Call your grandmother."

I did.

My grandmother asked, "Will there be a wedding this year? ¿Por qué no?"

"You're a Jehovah's Witness," I said. "You're not even supposed to celebrate New Year's."

I handed the phone back to my mother.

THE HOSTS HAD LINED the hallway with goody bags. I ended up getting one, too: a ceramic coffee mug and a box of chocolates. Later that night I will give the mug to my father and he will say, "Hey, thanks" and immediately chuck his old coffee mug into the kitchen trash bin, give the new mug a quick rinse, and place it upside down in the cabinet. Out with the old. In with the new. I will wonder: Is change this simple? My mother had already called my father, and he was waiting for us in the running car outside. "Let's go," she said. "I'll get our coats." But I busied myself, Saran-wrapping everything in sight: the leftover buns, the mustard, the pickles, the lemon squares, the cheesecake, the trifle. Then the chocolate-covered raisins, the raspberry thumbprint cookies and the Snickerdoodles, and the homemade fudge cubes from the lady who whispered in my ear, "I'm not giving up this recipe for anyone." I even Saran-wrapped the Fritos. My mother returned to the kitchen with her snow boots on, her coat not yet fastened. "Let's go already."

"I know, I'm coming, I just have to finish this."

"No, it's okay. They said they could take care of the rest. Your father is waiting outside. Come on. We can still make it to your tío's party." I pictured my tío Erwin and his Brazilian wife, their apartment stuffed with smells of cologne and rice and couples dressed up and moving to the beat of samba. The sleeping babies and toddlers collected in one of the bedrooms, the older kids fighting their eyelids to stay up until twelve, one, two in the morning.

The Saran wrap on the trifle dish was a mess now, and I had to start fresh. Next, I wanted to empty the ice bucket, dump the one ashtray (with Ft. Lauderdale written in cursive letters), toss out the crumbs in the bread basket, and place the single walnut brownie left on the silver serving tray into a Ziploc bag.

"¿Pero, qué haces?" My mother switched to Spanish. It was her way of saying: I mean it.

"Hold on." I wrapped the limp raw vegetables next, making sure to separate the carrots from the celery from the cucumber from the zucchini. I put these in the fridge, next to the small dessert dish full of mayonnaise that would be long left in the far corner of the shelf until Valentine's Day, when the Mrs. will have to make room for the heart-shaped strawberry frosted cake.

There was a line at the front door. The hosts distributed the last of the goody bags. The wall of cold whistled and threatened to come inside. I liked it. It was no longer snowing, and the air had a pink tint to it. My father waved from the car. My mother climbed into the passenger seat, paused, turned around and with her finger motioned the question, Do you want to sit in the front? I shook my head. No, it was okay. That month, January, I would begin to write my first novel. It would take a long, long time, but I would do it. That February, I would say goodbye to my ex-boyfriend for the last time. That March, I would go on a first date with my now husband, also a writer. For years I would continue to see Caitlyn, the world's greatest therapist, and I would understand a little better each day that I may not always be able to predict the temperament of the water, but I could build my own boat and, more important, steer my own boat. So that evening, or I should say early New Year's Day morning, I hooked my coat over my arm, my goody bag hanging from my wrist, and stepped outside. Even though my parents were too far away to hear me, I could hear me. And I said it aloud: "I'm ready to go."

GYMS

I MISSED SWEATING. I WANTED to run. I was living in Guatemala for several months, and my host mother, Blanca, told me that if I jogged around the neighborhood, I would look like a crazy person. "People don't really do that here," she said one Sunday morning as I tied the laces on my sneakers in the courtyard.

"Yes they do," her husband Alejandro said. He explained that people in Xela exercised, but they usually did it very early in the morning when the city streets weren't as busy with cars and people. I tightened my laces and told them I'd be back in an hour or so. They stared in silence as I left the house.

It was sunny and cool. I jogged slowly at first. Ah, yes. Running. Then, a whistle. Across the street a man grabbed his dick and called, "*Bella, bella.*" I quickened my pace. I felt that man's words all over my skin. Maybe running wasn't the best idea in the middle of the morning when the city was packed with slimy, dick-grabbing men. I switched to a power walk. I had to pay close attention to where I stepped. Dog poop, deep potholes, uneven sidewalks, cars, motorcycles, and enormous buses that pushed me up against buildings, threatening to run over my feet—all that made for a stressful walk instead of the soothing calorie burn I had been seeking.

So the following week I visited a couple of gyms, *gimnasios*, one of which was essentially a petri dish of germs in the form of three weight machines, two benches, and a skinny guy reading the newspaper at the front desk while half a dozen men lifted weights and stared at their reflections in the rusted mirror; the second gimnasio consisted of a long, narrow room on the third floor of a building in a neighborhood I would likely never find again seeing as how there were no numbers or street names in that zone. Discouraged and desperate as ever, I *needed* to find a gym. It wouldn't be the first time I felt that particular angst in a foreign country. My obsession with gyms started with my introduction to dieting. And that started when I was a child.

DIETS WERE ALWAYS SOMETHING white women did—women my mother cleaned houses for in the wealthy suburbs. These women would take Dexatrim diet pills and sprinkle artificial sweetener from pink packets onto grapefruit halves. It was the eighties. They wore magenta headbands and leg warmers on their way to the gym. They carried water bottles. My mother—who came to this country from Guatemala weighing one hundred pounds and, like many immigrants, discovered that Big Macs cost less than a packet of vine-ripe tomatoes—gained ten, twenty, then thirty pounds, eventually reaching nearly double her green card weight. She joined the new gym down the street from our house, Futura.

The first time I went with her at the age of twelve, I stepped past the racquetball room, where dripping-with-sweat men looked to be in great pain as their sneakers screeched loudly in the narrow space. I was scared. What if that small blue ball smacked them right in the face? And I was entirely unprepared for what I was about to see upstairs in the ladies locker room. Never had I seen naked women in real life. The occasional sex scene in movies I wasn't supposed to watch—*Dirty Dancing, White Men Can't Jump*—revealed nude women's backs and chests, but never below the waist. The locker room ladies had nests in between their legs. They had cellulite on pale thighs, dark rings around their middles where the fat sat, and bumpy brown nipples. After that abrupt introduction to the female body, I began waiting for my mother in the carpeted hallway outside the locker room while she changed her clothes. Then I'd sit cross-legged in the corner of the workout studio, a pink notebook on my lap, writing stories about girls with spiral perms, while my mother stepped sideways and spun in front of the mirrored wall along with a dozen other women wearing leotards. It looked fun.

It didn't work. My mother eventually canceled her gym membership. But I, on the other hand, had barely turned page one of what would be a much-treaded path.

I was an A student. My group of friends and I were the popular girls in our elementary school's sixth grade. I was great at calligraphy, and I'd made the chorus group. My friends and I would meet at one another's houses on Saturday afternoons and take curling irons to our hair and eye shadow to our lids, trading jean jackets and vests. Sometimes we'd meet spiked-hair and Samba-wearing boys at the movie theater, although none of us had an actual boyfriend. Then, one day, everything changed. At school one day I stood in line with my Trapper Keeper on my hip as usual. I wore jeans and a checkered sweater, with my hair pulled into a thick side ponytail. The boy behind me was laughing. What was it? What had I missed? That was my first reaction, for I was always on the good side of a joke, on the side that other classmates envied. The scrawny blonde boy, Peter M., continued to laugh. This time it trickled down the line as we waited for our teacher to give us the signal that it was time to move to the next classroom for science. What was it? Peter M. cleared his little pink throat. You look like a soccer ball, he said. Immediately my face burned. The giggles I heard down the line fanned this heat, this horror and shame I felt in my body, because of my body.

Not long after that, I used money I'd earned from babysitting on the *Jennie Garth's Body in Progress* VHS tape. On its cover, the (popular, blonde) actress leaned against a piano with a gray sheet draped over it. She wore a black sports bra and spandex shorts. Her shoulder-length hair was blown out and teased in a "natural-looking" way, and her red lipstick matched the color font used for the subtitle: *Jennie Garth of Beverly Hills 90210 Introduces Her Own Personal Fitness Plan*. I bought the tape because I actually believed that I could be transformed into a likable version of myself. The day after I bought the video, I jumped off the school bus and climbed the driveway to my house. I dug out the key we kept in a secret spot in the wicker blinds inside the front porch and opened the door. Then I sat on the living room couch while I played the tape in its entirety. I wanted to understand the sequence, study it, before I completed it every day for the rest of my life. What did I wear to exercise? I don't remember owning any "workout clothes." What would that mean for a twelve-year-old anyway? Kids—even preteens—didn't work out; we played. Or, we participated in sports. For me, that meant half a dozen soccer seasons and one pathetic winter of Saturday mornings spent at gymnastics class, where I watched skinny girls flip and balance and tumble on bars and beams while I practiced somersaults on the blue mat. Jennie Garth's fifty-minute workout video, I believed, would really work. My five-foot body carried the evidence of years of unmonitored grade school snacks and endless bowls of sugary cereals with whole milk on weekend mornings, not to mention seconds and thirds of *tres leches* birthday cake and store-brand Neapolitan ice cream at family parties.

At home my sisters and I were never allowed to open cartons of orange juice, bags of chips, or packets of Kraft sliced cheese without our mother's permission. My mother kept a close eye on these glossy packaged items. In Guatemala, she and her six siblings ate tortillas and black beans most nights of the week. After school our mother always called us from work. That's when we'd fire off our questions: Is it okay if we open the fruit punch? Please, can I open the cookies? Silence. "Bueno," she'd say. "But don't eat them all." For that, she'd yell, "What! I just bought those cookies. What do you girls think—food is free?" So began the guilt surrounding food. Under my bed or downstairs between the couch and the wall I would hoard plastic cups full of Doritos, mugs full of rice, and the occasional bag of Cheetos. I vaguely understood that too much food made one fat. Back then I had no notion of calories. Or, I didn't care. Or, at least I didn't think I cared when I was slicing bananas that I'd dip in sour cream and sugar.

Skipping breakfast was easy. At lunch I ate only strawberries. Some days I'd add a few crackers. It became addictive, this game. How little could I eat? One day all I ate was an apple-flavored

Nutri-Grain bar. I felt so proud of myself, more so than when I earned high honor roll or when I first got paid for a babysitting job. I felt powerful and in control. By the end of seventh grade, I'd mastered the one-meal-a-day diet. Not eating anything all morning and afternoon, I'd return home from school and eat whatever I wanted. Because my stomach had shrunk, I never ate too much. Maybe I'd eat a plate of spaghetti and meat sauce or a ham sandwich and a salad with dressing. Then I would go for a three-mile walk. If I missed a walk due to rain or an orthodontist appointment, I would walk six miles the following day. Like this, I managed to lose ten, twenty, and eventually thirty pounds. By the time I started eighth grade, I'd stopped getting my period and my hair began to collect in thick bunches when I brushed it. You look great, relatives would practically cheer (except for my Dad who said I looked green). Once, my math teacher stopped me in the hall and placed his freckled hand on my shoulder. In his coffee breath he told me, "You look good, kid!" The praise from adults and the recognition from even more popular girls with even higher hair-sprayed bangs, not to mention boys in the junior high hallways, were new and gratifying. Delicious.

KERRI, THE PROGRAM COORDINATOR at the school where I was study- ing Spanish in Guatemala, suggested I try out Scandinavia Gym. "Don't expect anything too-too fancy," she said. "I mean, but it's clean. I go there."

To get to Scandinavia Gym, I walked from my neighborhood to the nearest microbus stop at Parque Bolívar. There I waited for ten minutes. Finally a microbus rushed past, slowing down just long enough for passengers to crawl inside the already cramped minivan. The *ayudante*, who looked to be about twelve, ushered me inside. His job was to call out the names of destinations, collect the coins and bills from passengers, and make sure no one cheated the driver out of a fare. Children paid too. If you had a big bag, you paid extra as well. Inside the microbus I sat pressed against strangers. I tried to be patient when the already crowded van stopped to pick up more passengers. Almost forty minutes later the driver pulled up in front of the shopping center across town. From there I walked another ten minutes along the busy street until I reached Scandinavia Gym. I stared at the mostly empty parking lots of the boxy buildings, stores with names I didn't recognize but ones that made me nostalgic for Macy's, Barnes and Noble, and Target. I fixated on the dozens of parking spaces outlined by white paint. I missed my car. I missed everything from back home.

It was a giant glass box covered with a gray rooftop. Behind it, swabs of cottony clouds brushed the tops of mountains. Inside the gym were a mix of Westerners and Guatemalans. The Guatemalans were all white. Women in decades-old-style leotards and sweat-bands on their wrists and foreheads pumped their legs and arms to techno music in the exposed upper-level studio. Men gripped iPods while power walking on the treadmills. Other men wore spandex shorts and towels around their necks. They strutted past me and ordered smoothies at the refreshment bar. My first time there, my eyes glazed over with pure delight at seeing the water fountain with a sign above it that read "Filtered Water." I signed up for three months. The membership fee was similar to that of a gym in Boston, but I didn't care.

That first day I ran like a gerbil on the treadmill. I sweat through my sports bra to the sounds of Usher playing through my iPod headphones while I dreamed of frozen yogurt and reduced-fat cream cheese on whole-wheat English muffins. I did the math as I pushed against the belt beneath my feet. The *pan dulce* I ate that morning: 200 calories. The mini-Snickers I ate on the microbus: 50 calories. A can of tuna with light mayo and two *tamalitos* from señora Carmen on the corner: 500 calories. I would need to jog at six miles an hour for seventy-five minutes, less if I ran uphill. By the time I left Scandinavia Gym that day, the sky was turning the color of a bruise. Otherwise, I would have run more.

The next day I returned to have my *evaluación*. It sounded scary. In a windowless office, I sat on a little red plastic stool while a woman named Emilia sat behind a desk and fired a series of questions she read from a clipboard.

"What is your motivation in joining the gym?" she asked.

Hmm? Shed this shell of flesh consisting of peanut butter, Snickers, and pan dulce? "Relieve stress," I answered. I felt bad that I was essentially paying dollars, *American* dollars, to sweat extra calories when the majority of the country couldn't afford to buy meat.

"How many days a week can you come to the gym?"

"Five," I lied. I would come eight times a week!

"For how many hours?"

"Hours?"

"Stand up, please."

I did.

The room's four walls (three white, one glass) were without posters. Emilia pulled out a measuring tape from one of the drawers. I swallowed. After six painfully scrutinizing minutes of her taking account of the width of my waist, hips, thighs, upper arms, calves, and chest, she recorded the answers on a chart. The last thing I needed was a ninety-pound Guatemalan woman, my age, counting centimeters of fat on my body. Thoughts crowded my focus. If my parents had never left their home country and I had grown up here, would I also weigh less than one hundred pounds? Was I just another spoiled American brat? Did Emilia think I was fat?

"Oh, wait," she said, reaching her arms behind me. We were close enough that I could smell her fruity lip gloss. Then she slowly wrapped the tape measure around my neck and ever so gently pulled.

THIS IMAGE IS AN apt metaphor for my relationship with dieting and exercise during this time in my life. In college I majored in international relations, in part because I wanted to travel the world, and wherever I went I always made sure to find a gym. My sophomore year in college I studied abroad in Vietnam. For four months, my boyfriend and I wrote long, sappy letters to one another that we mailed with foreign stamps on special airmail envelopes. I was nineteen. A group of American students and I lived in a dormitory for University of Hanoi students. We each had our own spacious dorm room with its own bathroom where I had to sit on the tiles in order to take a shower because the showerhead was not detachable and measured waist high. I liked the permanent stone-colored sky of Hanoi, the static-filled messages bursting through public loudspeakers at five in the morning, and the maze-like streets lined with cracked concrete buildings built during the French occupation. Sleeping under a mosquito net was romantic, old fashioned. After a while, the occasional run-in with a rat the size of a kitten didn't bother me, nor did the smells of urine or old fish sauce outside the dorm gates.

What did bother me: men on the street hollering profanities in Vietnamese, men on motorbikes pointing and laughing, men staring straight at my chest, women on the street snickering in trios, white-haired and wrinkled women in the park locking eyes on my butt when I walked past them. Or did I imagine it all? My American classmates and I compared stories over breakfast: scrambled eggs packed between two thick slices of French bread, sautéed cucumbers, and hot sauce. We laughed over enormous glass mugs of Tiger Beer or cocktails with names like B-52 or Sexy on the Beach. We always rewarded ourselves—for finishing a paper, making it to the market and back on our own, surviving a stomach bug—by going to restaurants. Our U.S. dollar stipend allowed us to live like the upper class in Vietnam. We could and did eat out every meal of every day. In between, we'd study in cafés or fancy hotel lobbies where we'd pinch off pieces of a pain au chocolat or Danish. We sipped coffee made with sweetened condensed milk while memorizing Vietnamese vocabulary from flashcards. One of my favorite cafés on Hoàn Kiếm Lake played American movies on Thursday nights. There, I'd order the breakfast platter for dinner. It consisted of a toasted bagel, peanut butter, granola, sliced fruit, yogurt, and honey. Sometimes I'd get hot chocolate too. I lived in wide-legged black pants, a popular style for women working in the markets or the fields in Vietnam. They were soft on my thighs and always fit, as they had an elastic waist. I didn't need to wash them too often either. I owned two pairs. A few weeks later—while existing in a sugary coma that carried me from meal to meal and letter to letter from my boyfriend in America—even those pants fit too tight.

I had tried, and failed, to walk to the lake as my daily exercise. The stares and run-ins with emaciated street dogs and the occasional toddler peeing into the open sewers along the sidewalk just became too much, not to mention the exhaust coming from the government Land Cruisers and zillions of motorbikes. So I tried running (okay, jogging) in the local park. Plenty of space. Still people stared, more so when my cheeks flushed from the effort, thus inviting more women in conical hats with blackened teeth pointing and laughing.

So I joined a gym at a fancy hotel. I spent half of my weekly school stipend on the membership. When my American classmates asked how much it cost, I lied. I did not want to deal with their judgment. My own guilt was enough. I was in Southeast Asia for God's sake! I should have spent every free hour practicing Vietnamese with locals, bartering in the fruit markets, and teaching little kids how to sing songs in English at the daycare by the lake. Instead, every afternoon I rode my bike in the Hanoi traffic to the hotel.

In the front basket I kept my gym bag (which was really just a white plastic shopping bag full of a change of clothes). The elevator lifted me to the top floor, where a young Vietnamese guy smiled and handed me a towel. On a corner-mounted television, MTV

Asia played Britney Spears's new video "Hit Me Baby One More Time." I was usually the only person there, so I had my pick of the three treadmills, one StairMaster, and two bikes. The carpeted gym and mirrored wall opened the space in a luxurious way. I could finally exercise in peace.

Aside from calorie burning, the gym was my haven. I'd traded the sounds of street men hacking up phlegm for the pleasant tune of the treadmill belt swooshing underneath my feet. No more teenagers coming up to me in the park and asking if I can teach them English, yes? No more waitresses playing with my hair. No more stares. In the gym I was by myself, with myself, in a way I couldn't be anywhere else. With each treadmill mile I logged, I felt closer to home. Closer to that buzzing, happy feeling I'd get during the previews at the movie theater. Closer to the rush of adrenaline I'd feel when I heard my boyfriend knock on my dorm door. Closer to the sounds and smells of home—phones ringing, meat sizzling, parents making plans for the day in Spanish. I ran. I examined my stomach and thighs in the mirror fifty times a day. I eyed my reflection in storefront windows selling incense and pig feet. I posed for pictures in front of temples with my hands positioned on my waist so my arms look thinner. I ran harder. I sweat until my underwear was soaked. Still, I was afraid it wasn't enough. Would my blonde boyfriend still love me? Would he notice the extra flesh around my middle when we tucked ourselves underneath the twin sheets of his bed? Would he use his long fingers to trace the pink lines my tight jeans left on my hips? And what about my mother? Would she pinch my arm fat at the JFK airport and give a disapproving smile like she had when I'd returned from Zimbabwe one

summer in high school? *I thought you'd come back from Africa smaller.*
The gym worked. I came back home leaner, stronger, *svelte*, as my
friend's mother said. I felt like I had woken up from a nightmare
the moment before being shoved off a cliff. Relief, relief.

AT SCANDINAVIA GYM IN Xela, the trainer Emilia tells me to step on
the scale. I pretended not to hear her.

"Step on the scale."

"No," I said.

How did I explain to this young girl, perhaps only seventeen
years old, that I had a strong aversion to scales? I put them in the
same category as dressing rooms. No, thank you. A specific number would send me swooshing down the mental slide of depression
for weeks, months, maybe longer. Do I tell her about the time the
physician's assistant announced my weight in the doctor's office
even though I had specifically told her not to tell me the number? How, afterward, I drove home in a panic—apparently three
pounds higher than the scale had said at home—and proceeded
to eat corn straight out of the can while watching a marathon of
Sex in the City episodes.

"I'd rather not know," I explained.

"*Vaya pues*," she said. "Just step on, and I won't tell you the
number."

I hesitated but did as I was told.

"How old are you?" she asked.

"Twenty-eight." I stared at her black sneakers. Her feet looked
like those of a second-grader.

"Height?"

"Five two," I said.

She squinted.

"Oh, in centimeters . . ." I tried to do the math in my head but it was difficult to concentrate. I could feel her staring at me, as if she had only then realized I wasn't really from here. I was a foreigner. I was different. I looked Guatemalan. I spoke Spanish. My name was De Leon. Yet, I measured myself in feet and inches.

"Sixty-two."

Next she had me do pushups on a blue rectangular foldout mat. I successfully did seven boy pushups before I collapsed on the thin plastic. Then I did squats. I was good at these. I could have gone on forever, but she had me stop at twenty-five. After she assessed me on sit-ups, flexibility, and one wobbly plank pose, I was released from the strange cell and instructed to follow her upstairs to the cardio section of the gym. She pushed a bunch of buttons on a treadmill, creating the beep-beep sounds I'd heard so many times in my life, beginning when I was thirteen and climbed a StairMaster for forty-five minutes three days a week after school at Futura Gym with my friends Hannah and Marie before we inevitably gorged on three-scoop sundaes and french fries at Friendly's afterward. I felt good. Alive. On my way. I walked uphill for five minutes while she excused herself. I tried hard not to think about all the other things I could be doing in that moment: tutoring children too poor to attend school, sipping coffee with my host mom, or writing a thousand words of my novel that had no plot, much less a title. Instead, I pushed the + button on the treadmill and walked faster.

I WAS CAPITAL-O OBSESSED with exercise. Even in Paris, where there was nothing to complain about—I could drink the water, I was happy—its chokehold still got me. One night I visited the Bar Hemingway in the Ritz. It was darker than I had expected. I stole the napkin, the rose from my Xin Xin Singapore cocktail, the coaster, and the menu. But then I put the menu back because I was scared someone would find out and deport me. The hotel lobby was sprinkled with wealthy tourists and loud businessmen. It may as well have been an airport lounge. But I liked looking at the display of photographs along the mahogany wall. One hundred and ten francs per drink, flower included. On the way out, a couple of Italian models linked their arms with men wearing suits. And I thought, if I didn't consciously concentrate on trying to keep my stomach flat during sex, I'd be a different lover. Years later, I'd recast those women as prostitutes in my memory.

My host mother, Madame Le Milon, was racist. "Les Arabes! Les Arabes!" She would shake her head while reading the folded newspaper each morning. At dinner I ate everything on my plate— roast chicken, potatoes, Camembert, salad with homemade dress- ing, torn chunks of a fresh baguettes. I drank wine. I accepted the slice of strawberry tart. After our meal one night, after Monsieur Le Milon had excused himself to go help their son prepare for bed, Madame Le Milon used the cloth napkin to wipe the corners of her mouth. In France, she explained, women do something called "faire le régime." What did that mean? She cleared her throat. "How do you say . . . eh, to diet?" I had the impulse to wave my fin- ger in her face and declare: *In France*, Diet Coke is more expensive than café au lait! *In France*, a salad comes with fried potato wheels and thick blue cheese crumbles. *In France*, wine is cheaper than water. Besides, a pain au chocolat never killed anyone, and it only cost five francs. But I knew what she meant. And after my internal defensive outbursts, I secretly agreed with her. I could be better. I could be smaller. I should be better. I should be smaller. Oh, Parisian women, with their silk scarves wrapped like snakes around their bony shoulders, their skinny jeans before they were called skinny jeans, their minimal makeup, effortlessly crossed legs on the metro, and leather purses that smelled like Chanel No. 5. Often I sat beside them. Whenever the train moved from above ground into the earth and I caught our reflection in the glass, I looked away. Thing was, I knew my body by heart anyway. On good days I'd see a small waist and wide hips, strong calves, size 8, a healthy woman's body. On the rest of the days I'd shake my head in disapproval—flabby triceps, thick thighs in need of serious squats to counter the extra hunks of baguette over the weeks.

One afternoon, after a lecture by Hélène Cixous at a building it took me an hour and forty-five minutes to find, I stopped in a café and dipped a baguette into sweet potato soup. Outside it drizzled. I was in a different arrondissement than usual. Madame Le Milon's comment stung like the sound advice you never wanted to hear. My pants weren't exactly *tight*, but the hems rose higher up my ankles whenever I sat cross-legged, and my bra fit snugger than usual. Across the street from the café, I noticed a sign for a gym: Lady Fitness. After I finished my creamy soup, I enrolled at the gym. But before that, I wrote in my journal once more: "Wouldn't mind lying in the sun with someone I love."

But, I mean, like, what was I supposed to do to faire la fucking régime? Take up smoking? Again, too costly. I needed to save my money for internet cafés and weekend Eurail trips to Florence, Berlin, Barcelona, and Amsterdam. I supposed I could have walked to class instead of taking the Métro. I could have woken up early and ran past the shopkeepers sweeping their storefronts. Or, I could have passed on the fruit tarts at dinner. But why would I? I was *in France!* I was twenty years old. I had decades of dieting ahead of me.

Head down in the shower I was allowed to take for five minutes only once a day according to the study abroad program rules (the French conserved their water more than Americans), I examined my toes while the water fell over my face, onto my shoulders, down, down, finding paths between soft flesh, into spaces that weren't there before quiche became *quotidienne* for me. That was it. I would work out before classes from then on, shower at the gym. Take as long as I wanted.

IN GUATEMALA, EMILIA, THE trainer with second-grade-sized feet, told me, "You are in the excellent category for cardio, average for squats and crunches, and below average for push-ups. You only have to lose about nine pounds," she said, smiling. Nine pounds! She was a liar. I knew I had at least fifteen pounds to lose, probably twenty.

"You're a little low in water, but not bad, and your muscle ration is actually only one point off. The pounds you lose and the muscle you gain will work together to get you where you need to be. If you come to the gym five times a week, while we really only recommend three, then you will likely reach your goals."

"Will I lose weight?"

"You must have a positive attitude."

I nodded. What a load of crap. "Thank you," I said.

"Para servirle," she said. Then she gave me a kiss on the cheek and left. Here I was, I thought, in Guatemala, a member of a gym that 90 percent of the population can't afford, nine pounds away from a magical number that I had waited and waited for like a hungry puppy. This number, I sickly believed, would set me free from years and thousands of workouts that I counted on leading somewhere opposite of here.

I PACKED THIS OBSESSION for diet and exercise, no matter how far I traveled, no matter where in the world. I remember the day I left for my summer internship at the United Nations in Lagos, Nigeria. I was twenty-one years old and standing in the terminal for the British Airways flight at Heathrow Airport to Lagos. In the crowded waiting lounge, I met a young couple. The woman, Victoria, told me that the baby wrap on her back was called an *ankara*. She and her husband were flying home. They suggested I try to get a seat near theirs. But weren't seats already assigned? All around me women wore gorgeous and bright kaftans and scarves tied around and above their heads. They matched turquoise tops with bright yellow zigzag patterns or purple polka dots. Others wore navy blue slacks and silk button-down tops. Most had their children clinging to them—dressed in their best frilly dresses for the girls and polo shirts for the boys. It was late, almost midnight. We would arrive in Nigeria when the sun was rising. "You will love Nigeria," Victoria said, "because Nigeria loves visitors." I asked her about clothing for women and then about food. What would I eat? Drink? Did I have to cook all the vegetables before eating them? Would I even cook? The African diet was carb-heavy. And it was the era of Atkins in the United States—not that the continent of Africa cared. I had only packed one pair of jeans. They would be my scale for the next two months. Long skirts and linen pants were great for the hot weather, but they were the enemy when it came to gauging how much weight I'd lost or gained. Would there be a gym I could go to after work? I'd be working at the United Nations Development Fund for Women. Did they have a sports facility for its employees? Maybe a track and field I could visit during my lunch hour? If not, perhaps I could power walk around the city blocks like I had in Manhattan the prior summer. In the row beside us in the airport lounge, a screaming toddler inhaled deeply before releasing a bubble of barf. His father caught it in his hands. Victoria adjusted her baby on her lap. "In Nigeria, you can wear whatever you like and eat whatever you want."

"Fabulous," I said, even though I knew it wasn't true.

When I was in Nigeria for the summer, reporting on women in development projects for the UN, I lived with a family on Victoria Island. On my first morning, the "house girl" Tessie served me coffee with sweetened condensed milk and oatmeal for breakfast. I hated the taste of bitter black coffee and so, even though I know condensed milk was high in calories, I added it to my coffee anyway. There was a slice of raisin bread on a plate. Raisins were dense with calories and sugar. I wrapped the bread in a napkin and carried it with me in my bag. Then the "house driver" took me to the UN offices located on another island. He told me I had my face pressed to the window like a girl child and laughed. We passed cars, smoke, and teenage boys selling everything from toothpaste to batteries to corn on the cob and a little girl with thick black eyeliner asking for spare change. I gave her the raisin bread. By the time I arrived at the UN compound, I was dizzy. There I shared an office with another woman who, after I asked her if there was a gym or something nearby, told me that if she ever tried jogging outside she would likely be raped and murdered and maybe have her tongue cut out to be used in a ceremony by the people who lived across the alley.

Oh.

At lunch I ate in the canteen with Chinwe. She was tall and had protruding cheekbones and liked to laugh. After I ate beef stew for lunch (the only item on the menu) and later unwillingly threw up in the bathroom, she checked on me every ten minutes for the rest of the afternoon before offering to ride with me back to Victoria Island. "Come now, let's get you settled before you change your mind and get on a return flight, *abi*," she joked. The next day she asked the cook to make me a special meal from then on: a plate of white rice with a greasy fried egg on top. Did they have ketchup? We can get some, she assured me.

Later I ask her if she could help me find a gym. She did. From that day on the house driver picked me up at five o'clock from the UN compound and took me to Proflex World Class Gym. He waited for an hour, sometimes an hour and a half, in the parking lot. Whenever

I stepped out of the gym, I was red faced and satisfied. Even though I spent my days writing reports and interviewing women involved in grassroots organizations that gave microloans to fishing communities and built literacy in the communities, or replaced a water well in a village, it was only after climbing a StairMaster to nowhere for forty minutes that I actually felt accomplished.

The gym in Lagos was on the first floor of a four-story concrete building. Treadmills and bicycles lined the long wall opposite the mirrors, making the gym seem larger than it really was. Iron bars in the shapes of hearts covered the windows. One corner of the room was dedicated to free weights. A blue bouncy exercise ball rolled gently between two hand weights. In the center, black and red weight machines were positioned only a few feet from each other. When I extended my legs on the quadriceps machine, my toes threatened to touch the man's scalp in front of me doing chest presses on the bench. Usually, there were only men at the gym. Maybe the women worked out in the morning. Maybe women here embraced their full figures and S-shaped silhouettes. Later I'd realize it was more complicated. Working out was a privilege like any other—it required time and money and cultural acceptance. Did the men and women collecting firewood in the countryside care deeply about their own cardiovascular health? Their body mass index? Their heart rate?

I WISH I COULD say that the obsession with diet and exercise stopped after college. It fizzled out, mostly after I had found yoga and therapy and gave birth to my son, but not before it got worse.

I was twenty-five, and for the first time in my life I could afford the best when it came to gyms and personal training. I'm talking two floors of a high-rise. Downtown, near the fancy hotels. Across from the oldest public library in the United States. High ceilings. Soft lighting. Dramatic split stairway. Three white Mac desktops in the lobby. A café bar that sold smoothies with soy milk and egg salad wraps made with fat free yogurt instead of mayonnaise. Spinach wraps. Protein bars. Personal television sets on each treadmill. Running at night and staring out at Copley Square, Boston, at other people living their lives while I challenged myself to run faster than six miles per hour. Pilates classes. Spinning. Kickboxing. All required little laminated tickets you got at the curved reception desk beforehand. Instructors with headsets. Women in matching exercise clothes. Women in flats, expensive sneakers, high ponytails, listening to iPods and holding Starbucks coffees in their hands. A full spa. A daycare. Me burning up to one thousand calories in a workout. Me going twice a day some- times. Me almost fainting, ripping open an Odwalla bar in the lobby and chewing it like an animal. Fluffy shower towels. Fluffy smaller towels for sweat. Private lockers. Free Q-tips. Lotion, shampoo, conditioner. Cotton balls in square glass jars on the vanilla countertops. Softer lighting in the dressing rooms. Pastel- colored flyers taped behind bathroom stall doors advertising 10Ks for breast cancer awareness month. Cucumbers for my eyelids while I sat in the sauna and the Jacuzzi. It was the first time I had worked with a personal trainer: "You poor thing, you got me after an espresso." We did squats, hammer curls, triceps dips, something called burpees. Once, I called into work and told them

I'd be late. I had a car issue, I'd said. Instead, I went to the gym. When I showed up at work, freshly showered and smelling like peppermint lotion, my boss called me into his office. I felt the heat in my cheeks spread to my neck. That night I called a therapist. My first time.

A month later, on my way out of my new therapist's office in Back Bay, she stopped at the door and asked, "What do you really want to be doing right now?"

It was a gray, humid day in Boston.

"Writing in my journal at a café on Newbury Street and drinking an iced coffee," I said.

"So why don't you do that?"

"I have to go to the gym."

She looked down at her red-polished toes. "Who says you *have* to?"

"Me."

SO THIS MIGHT BE the part of the essay where I tell you that therapy saved me and that with a dozen self-help books and journaling and learning to enjoy exercise for the pure sake of it, I was cured. Of course, it is not that simple. In Guatemala I continued going to Scandinavia Gym every day. When I came back home to Boston after living in Quetzaltenango for several months, I immediately joined a gym. Over time I have had other demands compete for my time and energy, among them family, work, writing, and taking the dog to the vet. On a practical level, I had less time to devote to the crazy. Again, not that simple. So much of the chasing and seeking and sweating had to do with, I now realize, so much more than numbers—calories, miles, steps—and as much to do with the recognition that there were times, plenty of times, when I felt the weight of darkness, that nothing I did was enough, that there was always better, and better was always smaller. But I realize now this logic is dumb. In my best moments, I do not so much see sweat as my drug and the gym, my dealer. In my best moments, I do not think about it at all.

Still, today, almost a decade after that weekend morning I attempted to jog in the streets of Quetzaltenango before enrolling at Scandinavia gym, I must pay close attention to where I step. I try not to weigh myself every morning. I try to take vitamins and drink plant-based protein shakes with chia seeds. I try to exercise for health, not vanity. Maybe that really only means I rationalize the cost of my fancy heart rate monitor and membership to a big, boxy gym that has its own hair salon and day care and café and plenty of parking. And I love it. Yet, on days I can only do one, I almost always choose to bring my laptop to a coffee shop rather than pound the treadmill with *have to* and *should*. Instead, I look ahead to Sunday yoga classes, ones with names like "Surrender."

THE STORY OF THE LETTER
FROM MY FATHER

HAVE TOLD THIS STORY before: How when I was in ninth grade, my father ran away from home. How one frostbitten New England morning, he climbed into his gray Toyota—the one whose passenger door didn't open from the outside—and drove toward Guatemala. I tell this story when I am giving readings or lectures or talks at schools, libraries, bookstores, or universities. Even to my own students. I notice how people stop fidgeting and put down their phones. The energy shifts; it settles. The audience is *in*.

I TELL THEM HOW my father left a letter for my mother on their bedroom bureau telling her he was done with America, that he was tired, that he was leaving us, going back home to Guatemala. He had written the note on a piece of my pink paper. I describe how, initially, I was bothered that he had used my Lisa Frank neon notebook without my permission. Someone in the audience usually laughs, for which I am thankful.

I EXPLAIN HOW THAT week I went about my fourteen-year-old life as usual: volleyball practice, hanging out with my boyfriend, babysitting, all while my mother had hushed conversations on the telephone behind closed doors. I explain how somewhere around Washington, D.C., my father turned back. How one Friday night, when I was on my way out the front door—going to the mall with friends or off to babysit, I don't remember—my younger sister was watching cartoons in the family room, and beside her, sat my father, still wearing his coat, tears streaming down his face.

AT THIS POINT, A lady in the audience usually covers her mouth with one hand.

I THEN SAY HOW my family and I never talked about this tear in the fabric, this rip in the seam. Ever. It was as if it hadn't happened, as if my father had not, momentarily, chosen a country over his family.

HIS DEEP-ROOTED YEARNING FOR his homeland has haunted me ever since. What if he had kept driving? What if he had made it to Guatemala? Started a new life? A new family? Even in the hypothetical: Did he miss us? My father, who lives fifteen minutes down the road from me now, my father who has been homesick for over forty years. Why wasn't the American Dream enough?

THE WONDERING GREW TOO big to hold, and so, I tell the audience, I am the one who left this time, to Guatemala. I took these questions with me on my trip there. I took them on the plane, and I took them to the page. In fact, I wrote an entire novel based on a man who wants to return to his homeland, but his wife does not. I wrote stories and essays and a couple of poems based on these questions with no easy answer. Typically, this is when I launch into one of them. The audience shifts in their seats. The woman whose hand was on her mouth now places it on her lap. And the sound of my own voice in the microphone at the podium startles me, no matter how many times I tell this particular story.

MOTHER TONGUE

EARLY ONE MORNING, A few minutes past six, I stumbled into my two-year-old son's bedroom, and as I lifted him out of his crib, he announced, "I want meatballs." This was just after I had said, "Good morning, mi amor." Had he not heard me? "You want meatballs?" I asked, just to be sure. He was wearing his favorite monkey pajamas. "Sí," he said. At that moment, like any moment when he speaks Spanish, where a Spanish word instead of an English one escapes his little mouth, I instantly feel a fierce floating happiness, that all is right in the world and in my life and his life or at least in that sentence, "Sí." In those moments, he could ask for anything, and I would probably give it to him. Meatballs at 6:00 a.m. Why not?

My first language was Spanish. Or, so I've been told. When I was a young child, my family and I spoke only Spanish at home. It was my older sister who brought English to our two-bedroom apartment in Boston. She was the one who diligently did her worksheets and packets of homework while seated on the plastic-covered couch. Once, I asked my mother why she didn't know the answer to one of the worksheet questions, but my sister did. You're old, I said, as if old people knew everything there ever was to know, as if learning stopped at a certain point, like growing in height. My mother laughs when she tells this story.

After English invaded our home, displacing Spanish word after Spanish word—first through those photocopied packets and later through television and eventually my own crinkly covered library books—Spanish became the stepchild language. I didn't want to play with her anymore. She was weird. Cartoons were in English. Movies too. We heard English at the mall and the doctor's office. So my sister and I spoke mostly in English. When my parents talked to us, which was always in Spanish, we replied in English. Then, we moved to a town twenty miles west of Boston where my parents bought their first house. My dad built a fence, painted it white. Bit by bit, episode after colorful cartoon episode, grade after grade in my sunny suburban elementary school, where it seemed everyone spoke in English, even the mailman, my world continued to be eclipsed with the sounds and songs and sayings of English.

The summer I was nine years old, my parents took us—by then there were three of us, all girls—to visit Guatemala, their homeland. I can practically sip those sensory details through a straw. Thin cucumber slices sliding in bowls of lime juice and salt. The smoke-filled streets as we squatted in the back of an uncle's pickup truck and swished past the city and onto dirt roads bumpy as logs. The sound of iron gates opening and closing, people everywhere, in and out, hola, adiós. Then, a sudden longing on my part: how I wished to move between two languages! But my Spanish was nearly lost by then. So in Guatemala I used English whenever I could, and when I was absolutely forced to speak in Spanish—say, to my thousand-year-old tías—I would do so with hunched shoulders, a lowered chin, furrowed brows. Painfully, the words would crumble out, and with them, my aunts would giggle like girls. I clumsily chopped verbs, failed to use the subjunctive properly, addressed elders with a casual *tú* instead of *usted*. So I began using Spanglish. And I can't say I have ever really stopped.

On that first trip to Guatemala, to the land my father still longs to return to someday, to the home my mother carries in her heart but vows never to inhabit again, I found other ways to communicate. I used gestures or made up words like "watchear" and "la ketchup." Or I begged my older sister to translate. She had a tighter grip on Spanish, perhaps because she was the firstborn and had more time to absorb the sounds and rhythms of the language before I came along. During our visit to Guatemala, my parents, it seemed, were around but not available. Either they remained plugged into hushed conversations around the table at night, adults sipping black coffee in which they dipped torn pieces of *pan dulce*, or they were totally unreachable in the midst of back-slapping laughter with neighbors and relatives they hadn't seen in over a decade. So I was left to fend for my own words in which to express what it was I wanted.

What I really wanted was to start fresh, to learn a language that was mostly my own, and not to subject myself to the burning humiliation of getting a word wrong in Spanish. So in sixth grade, when students were asked to select one language elective—French or Spanish—I imagined myself grabbing fistfuls of French words like a gambler extending his arms across a felt-covered blackjack table to collect his winning chips. I was greedy. I wanted three languages, I said. I wasn't yet aware that I would always mourn the days when I reached only for words in Spanish, for the nights when I dreamed effortlessly in Spanish. Back then, though, I rationalized, it wouldn't matter—I was learning French!

In college, like in high school, I excelled in French and ended up double majoring in international relations and French studies. I could easily write a five-page academic paper in French and pass an oral exam. And during my junior year, when I lived with a family in the 15th arrondissement of Paris, I could argue with my six-year-old host brother in French. He liked to jump on the mustard-yellow leather couch in the high-ceilinged formal living room. Arrête! Arrête maintenant! I'd say, without trying, without making those mini-bridges of translation in my mind before my lips moved. French came easier to me than Spanish.

Sometime in my twenties I read on a magnet, What would you do if you just gave yourself permission? The question throbbed in my subconscious, or my brain, or my heart, or wherever these questions live and feed and eventually demand your attention. What would I do if I could just give myself permission? I had never gone to Guatemala by myself, alone. So I gave myself permission to learn, or perhaps relearn, Spanish. I read, wrote, listened, spoke, and, yes, eventually dreamed in Spanish.

During the immediate years that followed, I would return to Guatemala again and again, even getting married in the old cobblestoned capital of Antigua, surrounded by friends and family, in English and Spanish and, of course, those languages that transcend words—food, music, dance. By virtue of being fluent in Spanish, particularly as an adult, I experienced my surroundings differently. No one giggled at me. Instead, I found I was able to speak of politics, women's rights, and the cost of chicken. I held this new relationship to Spanish so tight, gripped it in my palm, my fingers curled around it. I belonged.

Later, back in the States when I was pregnant with my son, like many expectant mothers I read everything I could about the "growing life inside me." Blogs, websites, articles, books. This was my first pregnancy, and I was deeply aware of its biology and its magic. I had read about the benefits of expecting mothers singing to their babies in the womb, talking to them, reading to them. My own mother urged me to speak to the baby in Spanish. And I did, but with skepticism that the short phrases and occasional conversations wouldn't be enough, that, eventually, English would swallow any crumbs in Spanish whole, like it did me. I gave up before I had even tried.

Once my son was born, and I mean the second the midwife thrust my son's slimy body onto my chest, I cried. That was the first language, my animal language. Then I said, "Yo te quiero." I love you. My first words to him needed to be in Spanish. I didn't plan this. I didn't know in advance what I was going to say, not say. But then, after dunking him ever so briefly onto my chest, the midwife passed him like a football to a nurse who whisked him across the room where a team of doctors poked him and tapped him and used a suction thing to eliminate the liquid in his mouth and lungs. I yelled to my husband, who was hunched over our baby, "Talk to him!" I watched all this from my delivery bed in the hospital, never doubting that my baby would live. Instead, what I worried about in those first minutes of his life had to do with words and sounds. The nurse's Boston accent, "Come on, honey, you gotta push!" The doctor's doctory language. The voice on the intercom paging a surgeon. The sound of the air conditioner buzzing. The early morning birds cawing in the distance before the metal and rubber of traffic muted the sounds of nature. It was all wrong. My husband needed to speak to our son. My son needed to hear him, us. And he did. And our baby woke up, mad and wet, crying and wailing. Animal sounds.

A few weeks after he was born, after the foggy, hormonal, timeless stretches where I traded the ability to sleep, eat, pee, or shower for those indescribable nose kisses with my newborn, I could finally think again. One thought: he is growing so fast. The next: he needs to learn Spanish right now, while his brain is a sponge or whatnot. Hurry, hurry! We have to download nursery rhymes in Spanish, I told my husband. And where are all those picture books in Spanish? The ones we had put on the baby shower registry? "I know!" I said, remembering a chapter I had read in some baby book. You speak to him in English, and I will speak to him in Spanish, okay? Okay!

That didn't happen.

We played a few songs, though.

During these early months when my son was an infant I attended a group for new mothers inside an old church on a one-way hilly street in Jamaica Plain. The group met once a week. Mothers sat in a circle as we held our babies in our arms or placed these warm cooing bundles onto baby blankets that we had stretched out onto the circle-shaped rug.

One particular Wednesday, I asked the facilitator to hold my son while I ran downstairs to use the bathroom. Sure, this is why I'm here, she said. So I reveled in the weightless journey down the hall and down the stairs, nothing in my hands, no bag digging into my shoulder, no need for a wobbly balancing act over the toilet where I always feared dropping my baby. No. I used the bathroom, took my time. I washed my hands! As I began to make my way back upstairs I noticed a bulletin board—yellow and blue fish, *pececitos*, painted onto white paper plates. Numbers, letters, shapes, colors, all in Spanish. A Spanish immersion preschool. I took an informational folder with me back upstairs, collected my baby, and hugged him tight the rest of the class.

I didn't read through the folder immediately. To be honest, at the time I couldn't imagine leaving my baby with strangers, not then, not in a year, two years, not ever. But even long before my son turned one, I felt the buzz of the preschool waitlist hysteria like an annoying mosquito in my ear. Sign up my son for preschool now? He can't even keep his own head up. I wasn't going to be one of those parents. I filled out the forms. Better to be safe. But then I blinked, and it was September. Time to go back to work. My son spent that first year with my cousin and my mother, and yes, she spoke to my son in Spanish, and yes, this made me feel less guilty for not speaking consistently to him in Spanish. Soon it was summer again. September. This time my now one-and-a-half-year-old boy would start school. Spanish immersion.

I admit, many days I wonder if he is too young to spend stretches of time away from his mama. The guilt is a cement cloak I wear most mornings when I drop him off and swallow the question: Will he be okay? That he is hearing Spanish all day from his teachers (native Spanish speakers), that the songs they sing and the books they read and the games they play are all in Spanish, this is what soothes me.

Still, there were two things I wasn't prepared for: the expensive tuition, and the fact that most of the other kids are white.

My family and I live in one of the most expensive cities in the country. I get that. Yet, what I truly didn't anticipate was that while learning Spanish day after day, my son would do so beside blonde and red-haired children who don't look like him, whose parents don't look like me. Does it matter? For me, the experience of speaking Spanish was always grounded in family, place. For my son, it will likely be associated with art, music, early friendships, and discovery. What will this mean for him later? For his identity? Will my son learn the kind of Spanish that sticks close to the bone, his core being, the way it does for me? When I lift him out of his crib and he asks for meatballs, is he coming off of a dream dreamt in Spanish?

I don't know.

The truth is, I want to protect him. Yes, I want to empower him with fluency in Spanish, his mother's mother tongue. But I want more. I want for him to be able to open and click that gate between languages with total confidence, never hunching his shoulders to embarrassment, shame, for forgetting where he started. I want him to keep this tradition alive for his kids and their kids. For all of us. And, yes, I want him to sit between the blonde and the red-haired children and feel at home in both languages. He is lucky to be learning in a time and space where Spanish is treated—mostly—like an asset and not a disability he must conquer, like testing out of an English as a Second Language track at school.

I want him to understand that Spanish is part of us, our family and our bond. I want him to feel that the words in Spanish are more than just an extra warm blanket piled on him at night but are an extension of my love for him, for who he is and who he will become.

BY THE TIME MY son and I make it downstairs, into the kitchen on this overcast spring morning and I prepare to take meatballs out of the freezer, he suddenly announces that he doesn't want meatballs, he wants yogurt. Okay, I say. Yogurt it is. Then, between yawns, I let the dog out and fill her silver bowl with food that makes a clang when it hits the bottom of the dish. Reach for a mug. Grind the coffee beans. Above the noise, I hear a small, sugary voice that requests, "Más, please." My son. Mi amor. And I give myself permission to leave words behind momentarily, think not of the day and its many tasks ahead and instead listen in the distance for the birds that fly in wind that has no language.

BRIDGED

OR SEVERAL SUMMERS SPANNING over a decade, I taught in a creative writing fellowship program for talented teens in the Boston area. It is a competitive program, and over the years many students have stood out, but none quite like Patricia. While the majority of other students were white, upper class, and often attended private schools, Patricia was Latina, an immigrant, and attended public school. Like me, she also had long straight black hair and caramel skin, and she was the first writer in her family. That particular summer, the fellowship's culminating reading took place at the gorgeous Athenaeum library near the Massachusetts State House on a humid Thursday evening in July. The teens had been prepping for it—timing their readings, perfecting their performances, filling up on greasy slices of pizza before changing into summery dresses and button-down shirts and ties. Family and friends were meeting us there.

Right before the reading, Patricia handed me her cell phone in its glittery blue case. Her mother and sister were on their way from Brighton, but her mother didn't like to drive in downtown Boston. She was running late. Could her mother call me in case she became lost? I knew her predicament well. Event about to start. Parent not yet there. Heart racing. This was a feeling I often had in the past. My mom hated driving in the city too. My mom was from another country too. But I had no idea if Patricia's mother would show up in time and what I would do if she didn't show up at all.

*

I DIDN'T GROW UP in a literary family. We delivered newspapers; we didn't read them. We told stories constantly, but we never wrote them down. My parents held blue-collar jobs. They worked double, sometimes triple shifts to pay for a house in a peaceful neighborhood with no speed bumps, where my sisters and I rode pink Huffy bikes around the sunny cul-de-sac during the summer.

It was during these summers that my mother collected back-to-school items for us. Bit by bit, the pile on *her* couch in the living room (off-limits to us) grew. We were allowed to use only the other couch and chair, and we never looked through the treasure collecting on her couch. Perhaps my sisters and I believed the pile would disappear if we touched it. Sometime during the last week in August, when my sisters and I couldn't take the anticipation anymore, she would call us into the living room, and we'd sit in a circle. My mother would lift an item in the air—a lavender sweater, a sparkly headband, a new notebook, a packet of erasers in the shapes of tropical fruit—and toss them to us. By the end of the morning we'd each have our own small piles.

I treasured my back-to-school stuff as much as presents on Christmas morning. I inhaled the scent of new sneakers, ran my finger across the corduroy fabric of my new pants, and relished the sound of the metal rings in my new Trapper Keeper opening and closing, click-clack, click-clack.

School was around the corner, and only then were we allowed to wear our new clothes and to write in our new notebooks. Even at this young age, I knew my mother was different from other mothers. She did not volunteer to make heart-shaped Valentine's out of construction paper in my classroom or cut oranges into quarters and distribute them at soccer games. She was always at work. I knew my mother never had the chance to go to high school in her country, never mind college, but I also knew that she made her daughters thrilled for each September.

*

I DON'T KNOW WHEN it was exactly that I learned my mother worked as a housekeeper. She just always did. It was her job. Whenever I had the cold or flu and was too sick for school, I wouldn't stay at home. Instead, my mother took me with her to work. Once, in the third grade, I was out of school for almost a week with a bad cold, bronchitis maybe. It was a sunny week in January, and I went with my mother to each of her jobs. The suburban houses all blend together in my memory now, the smell of Pledge and Pine-Sol and the feel of dog fur on couches and the sight of enormous, worn leather shoes piled by the doorways: all of these are images that compete for space in the box of "mom/work."

That week I had my mother's attention. And the front seat in our family's maroon station wagon. At each of the houses I knew the unspoken rules. Don't touch anything, but if you must, return it to where you found it, doesn't matter if it's a book, a board game, or a doll; if you watch TV, make sure to put it back to the station you found it on before we leave; don't eat anything that can't go unnoticed.

I would always go straight to the kids' bedrooms. A teenage girl had stapled records on her ceiling. I wanted to do that. But I didn't have my own room, and we didn't have any records besides the ones my dad used to play on the stereo secured behind Windexed glass that only he was allowed to open. I wondered about these kids' lives, how they left their beds messy and open for a stranger to come and clean and tighten and tuck in corners of sheets, leaving them smooth and ready for another fifty hours of sleep until it all happened again.

*

THE FELLOWSHIP READING AT the Boston Athenaeum started. No call yet from Patricia's mother. I sat in the front row between my husband and the executive director of the writing center. Regie, the emcee, made introductions, his voice booming across the high-ceilinged, centuries-old space. Down the hall, hollowed white arches holding statues of dead white men echoed as far as I could see. Sleek wooden lamps dropped from the ceiling like long earrings. High bookshelves, balconies, oil paintings, small green lamps, the smell of oak and sun baked into crinkly books that looked like art, open and displayed on tall marble tables. Membership alone to this library was hundreds of dollars. Weren't libraries supposed to be free? I kept turning my neck, hoping that Patricia's mother and sister were seated in the back. They were not.

*

WHEN I WAS IN high school, my mother wanted to be in high school. She and my father enrolled in a GED prep course at the local vocational high school on Tuesday and Thursday nights. My sisters and I cheered them on as they left our cozy house and ventured into the cold dark during these mysterious pockets of the week. I tried to picture them there, sitting in desks in rows in classrooms where poster boards decorated the walls: the Monroe Doctrine, Manifest Destiny, Reconstruction. When they came home that first evening, or maybe it was after a couple of weeks, I don't remember, my father declared that the class was a waste of time and money and that they were both quitting. "What do you mean *we?*" my mother asked. She continued taking the classes and twelve weeks later she took the GED. We all prayed for her, especially my grandmother. My mother passed the test, and she used my older sister's white cap and gown from her graduation to take professional photos at Sears. I was so proud of her, but I also remember thinking: none of my other friends' mothers are only just now getting a high school degree.

*

I HAD MAJORED IN international relations so I could *travel the world*, something my mother had always wanted to do. On the eve of each trip, I would sit at the round wooden table in my parents' kitchen in Massachusetts and write letters to relatives and friends. When I was done, I always wrote a letter to my mother. This was the hardest one to write. What could I say to a woman who clipped coupons and stuffed napkins from Dunkin' Donuts into her purse so that I could have the chances she never did? *Dear Mom, thanks for everything. How could I explain that I wanted to become a writer, that for years I probably wouldn't make much more money than her? Dear Mom, Sorry I don't want to be a corporate lawyer.*

Traveling only solidified my want and need to write. Whenever the flight attendant handed me a long, narrow customs slip, I took joy in spelling *writer* inside the box labeled "occupation." After each trip I returned a bit changed. Nothing as dramatic as a shaved head. The changes were subtle, like those photographs taken of a person every single day for a year and when you look at them collectively, closely, you notice the slight sag of an eyebrow or perhaps a pimple.

My senior year in college, author Julia Alvarez visited my small liberal arts college in Connecticut. My English professor asked if I wanted to co-interview the award-winning author on stage. Of course, I agreed. For two weeks I read and reread her novels and essay collections, and I even organized color-coded questions according to theme: gender, immigration, the writing journey.

The evening of the event, I sat on stage and waited for her arrival. My professor was driving her straight from the airport to the campus center, where our interview was to be held under bright lights and facing a packed audience, which included my mother. People applauded when Julia Alvarez entered the room. She stepped onto the stage. It wasn't until that moment that I realized I had left my color-coded index cards back in my dorm room. I had nothing. Not even a pencil.

Afterward, at dinner, after the interview during which I tried my best to remember questions I had prepared and thankfully did well despite not having my notecards (maybe *because* I didn't have my notecards and therefore spoke naturally), after Julia Alvarez held a balloon wine glass of red wine in one hand and talked with the English department faculty, she wrote down her email address. "Let's stay in touch," she said. Then she proceeded to chat with my mother in Spanish. My mother even gave her a copy of an article I had written in a national magazine, my first published piece. I admit, I didn't believe Julia Alvarez would write me. But she did. We stayed in touch, and it was Julia who told me about the Bread Loaf Writers' Conference in Vermont. Over the next few years, every time I tracked her down at a reading she would say, "You should apply. They have scholarships," she'd insist. "Oh, and say hi to your mom."

Never had I felt so much the plugging in of two worlds: school and home, writing and family. I was so happy. But the feeling didn't last.

*

OVER THE YEARS, AS I increasingly pursued creative writing as a profession, there have been times when my mother didn't get why I would want to rearrange my life to spend two months in a Maine cabin with no TV or why I would be thrilled to have a story I worked on for years accepted in a journal that only paid in contributor copies. She wanted so much for me to be successful, and for her, a big part of that meant having a secure job, building a life where you don't have to worry so much about money. The writing life, at least then, didn't exactly fit this criterion. Her anxiety would sometimes bubble up in cold questions: "How much did you get paid for that story?" "What's going on with your book?" "That lady who wrote the Harry Potter books . . ."

I get it. She grew up in a country where educational opportunity was synonymous with economic opportunity. School, or having a formal education, was a way "out." Art, or artistic practice, was extra. Perhaps deep down her worry stemmed from protection. Who doesn't want the best for their kids? Nonetheless, I always tried to include her as much as I could, and she has always been there to celebrate my successes. After I won an essay prize from *Fourth Genre*, my mom carried a copy of the journal in her purse. She showed it to the women whose houses she cleaned. Thanks to her, more women in Wayland, Weston, and Newton have read that winter issue than if the editor had airdropped them from a helicopter into the Whole Foods parking lot. This was her way, I supposed, of trying to bridge the divide.

My way included writing about her and the rest of my family. I wrote essays, poems, short stories, novels, and even craft articles on how to write about the subject of family. Interestingly, my mother didn't always note the distinction between fiction and nonfiction. Once, when I wrote a story about a married couple, based on my parents but not actually my parents, my mother couldn't let it go. We were sitting on beach chairs on a rocky stretch of sand in Cape Cod. The sun was in my eyes. I couldn't see her face entirely. "Why did you choose the name Linda for me?" she asked.

"It's not you," I said. "She's not you."

"Well," she added. "I would never do that anyway."

*

DURING THE FIRST HOUR of day one in the Young Adult Writers Program summer fellowship, we did some icebreakers. "Go around the room and tell us something about yourself that we can't tell just by looking at you," I said. Some responses: I used to live in Canada; I speak Spanish; I have a peanut allergy. When it was Patricia's turn, she simply shook her head and whispered, "Pass."

Alright, I thought. *Some kids are shy*. I say "kids," even though half the class were taller than me, but as someone who has taught middle school and high school for over ten years, I was used to this. I was also used to getting the shy kids to open up—to peek out of their turtle shells.

Not Patricia.

That whole first day she stayed quiet. When we shared our writing—quick character sketches, brainstorms, lists of things we hate—Patricia slid her blue-lined notebook toward me and asked if I could read it for her. Or she'd repeat, "Pass." That afternoon I spoke to her mother, in Spanish, on the phone. She assured me that her daughter was just really introverted. It was not a language barrier. Okay. First day jitters.

But it happened again the next day. And the next.

I admit, I was concerned. I paired her up with the friendliest teen in the room—which wasn't hard. Every last one of these teens also happened to exhibit *literary citizenship* without calling it so.

Patricia did the work. She filled her notebook. She even attended the optional write-in sessions on Fridays, borrowing a laptop from the staff office and typing up her work from the week. Sometimes in class she handed me notes: "I'm stuck."

Then came the odes. Patricia wrote an ode to the Dominican Republic. She was born there before moving to Boston at the age of two. Recently she'd gone back to the D.R. where she visited with dozens of relatives and rode motorcycles down muddy dirt roads, the wind whipping her long black hair. I know this because Patricia soon started communicating through photos on her cell phone. She'd show me picture after picture, one of her three-month-old baby cousin dressed as if ready for the prom, wearing a frilly pink dress and matching headband, and another one of her mom and ten-year-old sister, each wearing one-shoulder black shirts. I showed her photos of my then three-year-old son. *Bandido*, I called him. At that she smiled, just a bit.

*

CHRISTMAS MORNING MY JUNIOR year in college, my mother handed me a present. A white envelope. A gift card perhaps, I thought. Or, for more dramatic effect, cash. I opened the envelope to find a folded piece of paper. A printout of some sort. I read and reread it. It was my mother's registration for a college class at the local community college. I should have felt joy. Instead, panic set over my body like poured cement. She won't be able to do it. Not this.

In the moment, I congratulated her. Said it was a great gift. Wow. I tucked the registration back in the card. I tried not to think about the many ways my mother, ironically, hated writing.

She often asked me to write thank-you cards to employers for her and, years later, to write emails and texts on her behalf. She wrote in all capital letters. She was a good writer, a fine speller. But even her handwriting told me that it pained her, that she detested having to convert what was in her mind onto paper. She was a talker, a natural storyteller (that was her gift), but on paper she was shy, brief, to the point. And yet I knew she would need to write in this class. In primary school in Guatemala, my mother earned straight As. She was at the top of her class. But instruction was in Spanish. Even though she had learned to speak and read and write English once she moved to the United States at the age of eighteen, she never felt free on the page, in English anyway. I was scared for her.

*

BY WEEK TWO, PATRICIA and I shared books. I lent her a copy of *Drown* by Junot Díaz. Also from the Dominican Republic, he writes about the land, the people, and the dual consciousness of many of his characters who emigrated to the United States. I thought she might like to see familiar words and phrases and people on the page. And his writing is *really good*. I know I never had that feeling when I was young. It wasn't until college that I read books by Latino or Latina authors. I read *The House on Mango Street* by Sandra Cisneros for the first time my freshman year of college.

The next morning Patricia handed the book back to me. "You didn't like it?" I assumed the worst. "No." She shook her head. "I finished it."

Patricia worked on her ode to the D.R. and shared several drafts, both in workshop and one-on-one. While other students balanced multiple pieces throughout the fellowship—stories, poems, letters—like flaming batons in the air, Patricia steadily gripped her one baton. Her ode to her birth country.

*

AS MUCH AS I loved writing, it was almost always limited to my journals. I did not have an audience, never mind a writing workshop or a summer fellowship to develop my *craft*. But I had *ganas*. Grit, people might say today. And this, I am sure, came from my mother.

When I was twenty-eight and I had decided to quit my job—the one with great benefits and steady salary—and move to Guatemala to write a novel, my mother drove me to the airport; she even helped me cram a small printer and a stack of books into my red suitcase. Over the years I have invited her to readings, introduced her to other writers. Once, I even brought her as my plus-one to a writing workshop in Sicily when Bread Loaf hosted its first conference in Italy.

I have photos of my mother seated between authors Patricia Hampl and Michael Collier at a restaurant in the charming town of Erice in Sicily. I can picture her there now, reaching for the silver bowl of Parmesan cheese and using the little spoon to scoop the snowy flakes onto her plate of steaming shrimp linguini. What did others see when they looked at this trio? Who is this woman seated between these famous, respected authors? Why is she wearing a silver scarf and chandelier earrings? And, for me, it is a picture of my worlds merging. Why not wear chandelier earrings to dinner?

She made friends fast, charming the other participants during our shared meals. She took naps in the hotel while I workshopped my stories in an old church where, once, a palm-sized piece of paint from the ceiling fluttered down to the table during class. I still have it in a Ziploc bag.

Everyone loved her. It was the year my mother turned sixty, and this trip was also a gift to her. If I get to see the world through my writing, why shouldn't she? Deep down, I've always felt the adage *Lift as you climb* to mean more *Don't forget where you come from, bring your people with you.*

At the writing conference in Italy, we spent our free afternoons shopping for souvenirs and admiring the hand-sewn sewn lace napkins and tablecloths in the quaint shops. We took pictures. We spoke in Spanish. After the final reading, where one of the faculty read a piece about her dog and mixed in some musings on Montaigne, where my mother politely nodded and listened to the talk, the faculty member came up to me and said, "You are teaching us all how to be a good daughter to a mother." I smiled. She continued, "But, my dear, I kept thinking, what does she make of this Montaigne lecture?" She chuckled and walked away. I felt a pang in my chest.

Who cares about Montaigne anyway?

*

IN MY HAND, PATRICIA's cell phone buzzed.

Missed call.

It rang again.

I excused myself from my row and ignored my husband's

whispers, "What are you doing?" Yes, it was probably a bit unprofessional to leave the reading then. What would my other students think? That they weren't as important as Patricia? What did the executive director think? That I was picking a horrible time to use the ladies' room? Maybe this was all in my head. Either way, I left.

I waited until I got to the lobby to talk to Patricia's mother. She was lost and far away—somewhere on Newbury Street. I knew, looking at the glowing numbers on the cell phone, that even if she ran, she wouldn't make the reading.

Still, I stepped outside to the nearest intersection. City sounds competed for my attention. Where exactly are you? Right now? And now? I was a live GPS for Patricia's mother and sister. I talked her through the confusing Boston Common pathways and streets until I caught a glimpse of the two of them walking up the hill, the flash of light as it bounced off the balloon in their hands.

*

THE CLASS MY MOTHER took at the community college was a women's studies course of some sort. I have since then pushed away most of the details. I was in college myself, about to intern for the United Nations in Nigeria. I had just studied abroad in Paris. I was so naive. I thought I knew about the world because I had traveled some of it. Because I had read some books. Written some papers.

For my mother's final project, she had to write a twelve-page essay. I won't even pretend to remember the actual assignment.

I just remember the ugly way I avoided my mother's phone calls that month, how when I came home for spring break and she asked me to help her write the paper, I said no. I think I told her I didn't have time, that I had my own work to do over the break. I won't pretend to dig up excuses—I didn't have any good ones then, and I don't have any still—but I do understand my immaturity differently now. Maybe I was afraid she was hitting a wall, that she had reached the end of the dream, that the credits had begun to roll on her life and she was only now realizing it. Maybe, deep down, I was afraid that meant the camera now focused on *me*. The pressure of it overwhelmed me. What could I contribute to our larger Story?

That would be the honorable, well-brushed interpretation, wouldn't it?

But it's not the truth.

The truth is I was a coward. I didn't want to help her because I was afraid of seeing her limitations up close. I didn't want to see her fail. Why did I think she'd fail? Unlike the GED exam, this assignment was not multiple choice. Unlike other college courses, this particular class had only one written assignment: this paper. Writing, especially academic writing, I knew, was different from narrative and different from talking. My mother could talk her way—and did—through class discussions. She did not use the readings so much as evidence in her analysis but as springboards to share her experiences with and anecdotes about people she knew in real life. I knew that this probably worked because the course she took was a class for social work majors. But what would happen in other courses? After this paper would be another paper and another. What then? I was a hypocrite. I was sad. Even though I understood the divide between us, I didn't like it. I didn't want it to be there. A part of me wanted her to be like my friends' parents, the ones who emailed them feedback on paper drafts, the ones who forwarded them internship opportunities on Capitol Hill, ones who had car phones and used words like *indeed*.

In the end, she got a B. She came home with a white notecard that her professor had written on in cursive. I don't remember the exact comment, but it was positive. Of course, my mother carried the card in her black purse for days, probably weeks. Was I proud of her? Yes. Did she take another class? No. I don't think it is a tragic ending to the story. It's incredible that she took a college class and earned a B, that she attended the classes and did the readings, that she participated in discussions. She earned this accomplishment. What was so hard about my helping her? What was so hard about believing she could take more classes and earn a degree? I was living in my own movie, a narcissistic twenty-one-year-old, too busy to support my mother the way she needed it to succeed at the college level. To this day, it is a bit of an emotional bruise, like a question, like guilt. What if I had done more to help her?

*

JUST AS PATRICIA'S LITTLE sister and mother—dressed up, wearing white high heels, holding bouquets of flowers—crossed the street by the State House, my own cell phone buzzed.

Inside the Athenaeum, my husband sent me a text: the reading is over.

I pictured my own mother, pre–Google Maps, pre–cell phones, stopping at gas stations and convenience stores and asking for directions to the art museum or college center or hall where I was giving a reading. Sometimes she got there at the last minute. Other times she missed the reading, but we'd stage pictures to make it look like she'd been there the whole time. There is something so powerful in your parent seeing you do the thing you love most. Even now, when I see my mom in the audience at one of my readings, my fifteen-year-old heart within my heart beats a little faster.

*

I ONCE ATTENDED A reading by Esmeralda Santiago at the Harvard Bookstore in Cambridge. In her memoirs she writes about her difficult and complicated relationship with her mother, made all the more difficult and complicated after the family moved from Puerto Rico to New York City when Esmeralda was a child. The more Esmeralda became formally educated, in English, the more the gap grew in her relationship with her mother. I felt tremendous sorrow reading her work. I felt the same thing happening with my own mother. During the Q and A, I asked the author about her mother. "Has your relationship with your mother improved?" She shook her head. She even added, "It won't ever go back to the way it was. I no longer expect it to, and you shouldn't either." Or something like that. I was stunned.

After the reading, I stood in line and felt the weight of her twenty-six-dollar memoir in my hands, and when it was my turn I asked her to make the book out to me *and* to my mother. She looked up and squinted. I smiled. And I still had that smile when I left the bookstore with her book inside the plastic store bag, pushed the door, and stepped out into the fresh night air.

*

AS I STOOD OUTSIDE the Athenaeum, I sent texts like crazy. To my husband inside, to my co-instructors, to the program director. "Patricia has to read again. Stall? Two minutes away. Please."

Together, we solved the puzzle. Regie, the event's magnificent emcee, explained the situation to the audience and then performed a poem of his own.

My other colleagues sent me texts.

"Forty seconds away," I replied.

Finally, with shiny foreheads, Patricia's mother, sister, and I entered the packed room. A hundred heads turned toward us. I escorted Patricia's mother and sister to the front row, where they sat as Regie reintroduced Patricia to the podium. The clapping in that moment still rings in my ears. Patricia could hardly get through reading her poem without smiling or laughing or glancing at her mother, who beamed at her daughter onstage. Mother and daughter had the same long black hair and big dark eyes. In that moment, I felt they even had the same heart. Her mother reminded me of my own mother, not just because she was there, supporting her daughter, because Spanish was her first language, or because she had her arms full of flowers and balloons, but because her face wore an expression of unfiltered joy, with a shade of Where are we? How did we get here? Are we really here? My mother has had that look before, my mother who was born in another country and moved here for a better life. It is a certain look. And Patricia's mother had it.

*

I LIKE MEMORIES THAT are knots. Knots that are stories. Stories that are questions. They help me feel less like I need answers. Instead, I like seeing the patterns, the connections, the tropes and images and painful truths and limitations of our character, of time itself. I find comfort in the collecting, in the gathering of these seemingly disparate memories and, when possible, in making bridges between them. My story is part of a larger story. Everyone's is.

*

AFTER THE READING WE ate cookies and drank soda and took pictures. "Gracias," her mother said and hugged me. I realized I was still holding onto Patricia's cell phone in its glittery blue case. I tried handing it to her, but her arms were full—flowers, plastic cup of soda, a copy of my book I had signed for her, a helium balloon with the word "Congratulations!" tied to her wrist. Her little sister took the phone from me and giggled. It was contagious. I started laughing for no reason. Patricia's mother did too. Maybe it was the sugar, or the caffeine, or the adrenalin, or all of it. Maybe, I thought, writing is about so much more than what can be contained within the margins of a page. Maybe it's about what can be bridged. Or shoved together. At least for a moment.

I knew there would be times ahead when Patricia and her mother would feel the gap widen. In some ways, tonight was just the beginning of that break, of occupying different spaces, different worlds. I knew it was inevitable, just as it was between my mother and me. But it's okay. No, we can't (always) bring our mothers with us everywhere, even to the places they push us to the most—college, graduate school, workplaces, readings. But for me, that isn't (always) the point. The fear of leaving my mother behind, as I board a train going somewhere she's never been, will probably never go, is one way to look at it. Another way is to wave to her from the window, smile, and say, *Look how far we've come.*

ACKNOWLEDGMENTS

To the judges of the Juniper Prize for Creative Nonfiction, Madeleine Blais and Kathy Roberts Forde—thank you for your belief in my work. My gratitude extends to the entire University of Massachusetts Press team—Courtney Andree, Rachael DeShano, Nancy Raynor for your incredible copyedits, and Deste Roosa for the stunning cover. My book is home.

For your generous support during the years it took to write these essays, thank you to the Vermont Studio Center, the Virginia Center for the Creative Arts, the Bread Loaf Writers' Conference, Hedgebrook, the New England Foundation for the Arts, the City of Boston Artist in Residence program, VONA (Voices of Our Nation Arts Foundation), the Macondo Writers Workshop, and GrubStreet—the writing organization that changed my life, personally and professionally. I would also like to give a special thanks to Joyce Maynard for your friendship and hospitality and invitation to join the Lake Atitlán Writers' Workshop in San Marcos La Laguna, Guatemala.

Thank you to the editors and magazines who supported my work, especially Ryan Van Meter who selected "The White Space" as the 2012 *Fourth Genre* Michael Steinberg Memorial Essay Contest winner, Cheryl Strayed who listed "The White Space" as a Notable Essay in *Best American Essays 2013*, and Patricia Hampl who included "Mapping Yolanda" in her guest-edited issue of

Ploughshares in 2013. Huge thank you, too, to Ladette Randolph at *Ploughshares*, Khaled Mattawa at *Michigan Quarterly Review*, Kwame Dawes at *Prairie Schooner*, Jacob Newberry at *Southeast Review*, Dinty Moore and Joy Castro at *Brevity*, Jeanann Pannasch at *Ms.* (Thank you for publishing my first piece all those years ago when I was nineteen!), Kiala Givehand at *Generations Literary Journal*, and Erin Wilcox at *Drunken Boat*. Thank you, as well, to Stephanie Elizondo Griest for selecting "The First Day" to be included in *The Best Women's Travel Writing 2010*, Margot Kahn and Kelly McMasters for including "Mother Tongue" in *This Is the Place: Women Writing About Home*, and Deborah Santana for publishing "A Pink Dress" in *All the Women in My Family Sing: Essays on Equality, Justice, and Freedom*.

Mil gracias to Proyecto Linguistico Quetzalteco (PLQ) Spanish Language School in Quetzaltenango, Guatemala, and to my teachers there—*abrazos fuertes*, Maria Tulia—and to my host family, especially Blanca Perez. To Willy Barreno, friend and founder of La Red Kat (previously called Café RED) in Xela, and of course, César, for trusting me with your stories. And to La Casa Guatemala, for honoring me with the Rigoberta Menchú Award for an Outstanding Guatemalan Woman. I will continue to work to live up to that title!

Publishing a book is never possible without readers. Thank you to Alysia Abbott, Denise Delgado, Eson Kim, Alexis Rizzuto, Michelle Seaton, and of course, my beloved writing group, The Chunky Monkeys: Christopher Castellani, Chip Cheek, Calvin Hennick, Sonya Larson, Alex Marzano-Lesnevich, Celeste Ng, Whitney Scharer, Adam Stumacher, Grace Talusan, and Becky Tuch.

Endless thanks, always, to my amazing agent Faye Bender for your enthusiasm and wisdom.

To my colleagues, friends, and students at Framingham State University—you are all magnificent human beings and you inspire me every day. What an honor it is to be working in the very town (now city) where I was raised. Thank you as well to my colleagues and students in the MFA in Creative Nonfiction program at Bay Path University. And to Askold Melnyczuk, Dr. Miguel Lopez, Herb Kohl, and Julia Alvarez, Sandra Cisneros, and all the greats who came before: I am because we are.

Huge thanks to the amazing authors who offered generous blurbs: Julia Alvarez, Angie Cruz, Jaquira Díaz, Ru Freeman, Daisy Hernández, Alex Marzano-Lesnevich, and Grace Talusan.

I am also grateful to bookstore owners and staff, librarians, teachers, mentors, community workers—all of whom work tirelessly to put books into the hands of readers. *Thank you.*

Thank you, Guatemala.

Thank you, Boston.

For your love and unconditional support and for believing in my writing path even when it didn't always make sense—my parents, Dora and Luis De Leon. Thank you for your sacrifice, and your stories. To Karen and Caroline De Leon, my kind, hardworking, beautiful sisters, and to my extended family in the States and in Guatemala, including my amazing sister-in-law for building my website.

Thank you, as well, to my ancestors, my grandparents, the family I could not meet because circumstances of war, poverty, and dislocation caught us in different nets. And to all my friends—those who've been there from the beginning and those I've only recently met.

Finally, I would need a thousand hearts to express my love and appreciation to my husband—Adam Stumacher. Many moons ago, I prayed for you. And then you emailed me! And now we build our life together, with our two boys, Mateo and Rubén. For all this and more—thank you, God.